To: Jim, Madelaine & Jimmy

Our first step in this
journey is knowledge ....
It took great courage to
share this ...

Anne

Sept / 2002

Treaty Elders of Saskatchewan

Treaty Elders of Saskatchewan

Our Dream is That Our Peoples Will One
Day Be Clearly Recognized as Nations

H. Cardinal and W. Hildebrandt

UNIVERSITY OF
CALGARY
PRESS

University of Calgary Press
2500 University Drive NW
Calgary, Alberta
Canada T2N 1N4

Canadian Cataloguing in Publication Data

Cardinal, Harold, 1945-
Treaty Elders of Saskatchewan

    ISBN 1-55238-043-2

1. Indians of North America—Saskatchewan—Treaties. 2. Indians of North
America—Saskatchewan—Government relations. I. Hildebrandt, W. (Walter),
1951- II. Title.

KES529.C37 2000   971.24'00497   C00-911188-3
KF8205.C37 2000

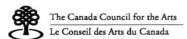 We acknowledge the finacial support of the Government of Canada through the Book
Publishing Industry Development Program (BPIDIP) for our publishing activities.

The Canada Council for the Arts
Le Conseil des Arts du Canada

Printed and bound in Canada by Friesens.
 ∞ This book is printed on acid-free paper.

Table of Contents

Foreword vii

Preface ix

Context 1

The Starting Point for Treaty Discussions 3

Shared First Nations Foundations 9

Iyiniw sawêyihtâkosiwin (The Peoples' Sacred Gifts) 10

Miyo-wîcêhtowin (The Principle of Getting Along Well with Others,
  Good Relations, Expanding the Circle) 14

Wiyôhtâwîmâw (The Divine Father) 18

Miskâsowin (Finding One's Sense of Origin and Belonging, Finding
  "One's Self" or Finding "One's Centre") 21

Kihci-asotamâtowin (Sacred Promises to One Another, The Treaty
  Sovereigns' Sacred Undertakings) 25

Wîtaskêwin (Living Together on the Land) 39

Pimâcihowin (Making a Living) 43

Tâpwêwin (Speaking the Truth or Speaking with Precision
  and Accuracy) 48

Askîwipimâcihowascikêwina (Setting into Place Arrangements
  for Livelihood, Living and Evolving Treaty Rights) 60

Conclusion: "... so that they may have a good future" 68

Notes 72

Glossary of Terms 78

Bibliography 81

Seven Treaty Elders Forums and numerous Elders Focus Sessions were held across the province of Saskatchewan with Elders from the Dene, Cree, Assiniboine, and Saulteaux Nations between 1997 and 2000. From left to right: Jacob Bill, the late Mrs. Toots Bill, Joe Stick, Agnes Alphonse, George Cannepotato, Allan Adam, Danny Musqua, Norman Sunchild, Gordon Oakes, Senator Jonas Lariviere, Bart Dzeylion, Alfred Billette, Miles Musqua, Pat Robillard, and Sterling Brass.

Foreword

As Treaty Commissioner for Saskatchewan, I have heard many different perspectives about the treaties in Saskatchewan. Most Canadians, I think, are aware that First Nations accounts of the treaties at times differ from those afforded by a review of written treaty documents. What many people may not know is that those differences, when carefully examined, can serve to strengthen our understandings of the importance, solemnity and honour that was forged into the treaties in Saskatchewan at the turn of the last century.

The eloquently timeless wisdom of the words that belong to the Elders of Saskatchewan, as transcribed in this book, provide invaluable contemporary and historical insight. The need for this book, however, originated out of other requirements. The Federation of Saskatchewan Indian Nations (FSIN) and the Government of Canada realized that the divergent paths they were following were not reducing the difficulties, frustration, and pain being experienced by First Nations people. In 1989, these two parties agreed to create an independent and impartial office which, at that time, would serve to research and provide recommendations on the issues of treaty land entitlement and education for First Nations in Saskatchewan. For this reason, the Office of the Treaty

Commissioner (OTC) was created. The original five-year mandate (which expired in March 1996) resulted in the signing of Treaty Land Entitlement Agreements between twenty-eight First Nations and the governments of Canada and Saskatchewan.

Based on that success, the FSIN and Canada decided to renew the office with a new five-year mandate effective 1 January 1997 to 1 January 2002. This new mandate was broadly defined and instructed the OTC to facilitate discussions between the FSIN and the Government of Canada that would strive to create common understandings on treaty rights and/or jurisdiction in the areas of child welfare, education, shelter, health, justice, treaty annuities, hunting, fishing, trapping, and gathering, and lands and resources.

Through an Order of the Governor-in-Council, it is my duty to guide the OTC through its new term. Presently, my role, and the role of the OTC, is to facilitate discussions about the meaning of the treaties and to work towards the implementation of their terms in a way that is consistent with the original spirit and intent of the treaties as it was, and is, understood by the parties. We are not here to negotiate new treaties, or re-negotiate the terms of the original treaties – these represent sacred

undertakings between the First Nations and the Crown that can not be altered. The OTC is an independent and neutral office that provides a forum for discussions between the Federation of Saskatchewan Indian Nations and the Government of Canada.

At the beginning of our mandate in 1997, our first priority was to get a sense of what the treaties were originally intended to accomplish, the manner in which they were created, and how the different parties understood the terms of the treaties and the treaty relationship. We asked historians from the academic tradition to research and examine the written treaties along with the historically documented accounts of events that influenced treaty making. Frank Tough from the University of Alberta, Jim Miller from the University of Saskatchewan and Skip Ray from the University of British Columbia produced an excellent synthesis of those written documents, giving us a detailed insight into the hopes, goals and pressures that influenced treaty making from the Crown's perspective. This, however, showed us only part of the picture. We knew that we had to ask the Elders to share some of their vast knowledge about the treaties in Saskatchewan. To this end, we travelled throughout the province of Saskatchewan, holding meetings in the different treaty territories to hear from the Elders who are the keepers of oral tradition and history. Together, the findings of these reports formed an integral part of the document *Statement of Treaty Issues: Treaties as a Bridge to the Future*, produced by our office in October of 1998, which highlighted the common understandings reached through our Treaty Table discussions.

The authors of this book, Harold Cardinal and Walter Hildebrandt undertook the task of working with the Treaty Elders of Saskatchewan to record the First Nations understanding of treaties and treaty making. The task was complex and time-consuming – complex because of the distinct First Nation languages (Dene, Nakoda, Saulteaux, and Cree), time-consuming because of the many meetings held to assess and discuss the numerous drafts produced by the authors throughout the process. Long, difficult discussions took place to ensure accurate translation and to ensure that sacred, spiritual beliefs and practices were respected. Yet throughout the process the Elders were patient but determined to see that their views were properly recorded. It was evident to all that the Elders wanted their point of view to be clearly represented.

The resulting material has not only been helpful in the Treaty Table discussions between the Government of Canada and the Federation of Saskatchewan Indian Nations, but the book is also an original contribution to understanding the foundations of treaty making across Canada. Other books on treaty issues have examined a wide range of issues, but no book to date has described the conceptual framework and theoretical foundations of First Nations treaty making. *Treaty Elders of Saskatchewan* begins with the First Nations belief in the Creator and the spiritual principles that emerge from First Nations creation stories. *Treaty Elders of Saskatchewan* then traces the ways in which the spiritual principles of peace and sharing are related to, and woven into, concepts of kinship, governance, and the right to livelihood. The book carefully follows the linkages from spiritual origins through to the doctrines that govern physical survival and daily life. Keywords and concepts that originate in First Nations language, such as *Miyo-wîcêhtowin ("Getting along well with others")*, *Wîtaskêwin ("Living Together on the Land")* and *Pimâcihowin ("Making a Living")*, are explained linguistically and phonetically to allow for a clearer and more comprehensive understanding of First Nations spiritual principles. An understanding of these foundational concepts, which emphasize sharing the land so that all benefit, as well as the related doctrines that describe the right to a livelihood for all peoples, is crucial if we are to build positive, forward-looking relationships based on the treaties.

Working with Elders is, in and of itself, extremely rewarding and enlightening. However, when such work requires knowledge of Elders with specific types of information, a knowledge of the protocols associated with requesting information of Elders is paramount. The Federation of Saskatchewan Indian Nations generously offered and, in fact, carried the responsibility of ensuring that the authors had an opportunity to hear from Elders representing all Treaty First Nations' linguistic groups and all treaty areas within the province of Saskatchewan. The tasks of identifying Elders with treaty knowledge, approaching them within the protocols of each Nation, requesting their assistance, providing translators, and ensuring their words were properly translated into English were only some of the important responsibilities undertaken by the Federation. Their cooperation in this initiative was truly invaluable.

At the heart of this book, I feel, is the notion that treaties are more than paper and ink as per the British tradition. Furthermore, the treaties are more than the exacting words that are passed on from the Elders of one generation to the future elders of the next generation. Historically, they served as building blocks for our country. Today, the treaties continue to shape how we, as the descendants of the original signatories, co-exist. This book reminds us of that significant shared heritage.

Judge David M. Arnot
Treaty Commissioner for Saskatchewan
October 2000

Preface

The Federation of Saskatchewan Indian Nations, Canada, and the Province of Saskatchewan (as observer) initiated a series of Treaty Elders Forums in the province of Saskatchewan. The Office of Treaty Commissioner, established by the parties to facilitate the process of treaty implementation, chaired the Treaty Elders Forums that were held in five treaty regions within the province.

Elders from each of the treaty regions participated at these open forums, making their presentations to the government parties and to the Treaty Commissioner. The meetings were open, with all participants being given the opportunity to make their presentations. At each of the treaty meetings, translators were present to enable First Nations Elders to make their presentations in their own languages. The translators then translated the presentations into English. These presentations were video- and audiotape-recorded.

The Federation of Saskatchewan Indian Nations provided the translators and Elder helpers, known in Cree as "*oskâpêwisak*." The Elder helpers assisted the Elders in the various ceremonies that were conducted in conjunction with these meetings.

Elders' focus sessions were organized with different groups of Elders where, again, meetings were either video- or audiotape-recorded. Transcripts were prepared from these meetings and used as primary material for this book.

As work progressed on the book, the Federation of Saskatchewan Indian Nations sent out translators to meet with Elders whose quotes were being considered for use in the book to seek both their consent to the use of their material and to verify the accuracy of the translations. More focus meetings were held with the Elders whose quotes are used in this book. At these meetings, initial drafts of the book were translated and reviewed on a line-by-line basis with the Elders. Each of the meetings produced changes, some editorial and some substantive, as Elders clarified those items that they felt had been lost, either at the initial presentation or in the translation. This book is very much a product of the Elders of Saskatchewan.

We tried in some areas to provide a context for the comments made by the Elders as a way of helping those readers who may not be familiar with First Nations. We were assisted in this process by a number of different translators, who had the very difficult task of interpreting some very complex and complicated First Nations concepts into English.

The translation was probably the most difficult part of writing this book. Some parts had to be translated a number of times until the elders were satisfied that their words and thoughts had been fully interpreted.

The result, we believe, is a text that contains a traditional First Nations theoretical framework to be used as guide for approaching the question of treaty implementation in Saskatchewan. What is unique is that, in the focus sessions, the theoretical framework provided was the result of a combined effort by Elders from the Cree, Saulteaux, Dene, and Assiniboine Nations.

The Elders were careful to point out that the framework they have presented represents, from their perspective, only the beginning. Much more work needs to be done with the Elders to examine in greater depth and detail some of the theories and concepts that they have outlined in a preliminary process.

In this book, we have used Cree words to describe First Nations concepts. The words are written in Roman orthography with the hope of making it easier to read the book. The Cree concepts described by these terms find parallel

Harold Cardinal

Walter Hildebrandt

expression in the languages of the Saulteaux, Dene, and Assiniboine peoples.

We were privileged to have had this opportunity to work with the Elders. We hope that the resulting book will better enable people to understand and appreciate the First Nations perspective.

We are especially grateful to each and every one of the Elders who attended and shared his or her knowledge and wisdom at the treaty table meetings, Federation of Saskatchewan Indian Nations (FSIN) Treaty Elders forums, and the Elders focus sessions. We appreciate the patience and kindness extended to us by these Elders during our sessions with them. We wish to thank in particular Gordon Oakes, Danny Musqua, Hilliard Ermine, Jimmy Myo, and Dr. David Ahenakew.

As well, we wish to acknowledge the unflinching and continuing support provided by the FSIN and in particular former Chief Blaine Favel, present Chief Perry Bellegarde, and Chief Irvin Star Blanket. We wish to acknowledge the support provided by Dr. Mary Ellen Turpel-Lafond, FSIN Legal Counsel (as she then was); Executive Director of the Treaty Governance Office Rick Gamble; Former Executive Directors Dan Bellegarde, Leanne Daniels, and Lloyd Martel; present and former staff of the FSIN Treaty Governance Office: Ted Whitecalf, Helen Semaganis, Nancy Demarais, Lori Bear, Brenda Manitoken, Carole Sanderson, Winston Walkingbear, Spencer Greyeyes, Anita Gordon-Murdock, Art Roberts, and Delbert Wapass;

and FSIN Communications staff: Jocelyne Wasacase and Lori Bateman.

In addition, we thank Mervin Dreaver, Allan Adam, Elaine Hay, Jerry Fineday, Ed Benoanie, Mary Ann Denecheze, Modest BigEye, Mary Rose Tsannie, Jim Roberts, Abel Charles, Jean L. Okimâsis, Margaret King, Eric Tootoosis, Roger Fox, Ted Robillard, and Marge Reynolds – all of whom assisted with translation.

The assistance of Albert Angus and Marian Dinwoodie (provided courtesy of the Federation of Saskatchewan Indian Nations) and Tracey Robinson, Sheldon Krasowski, and Darrell Seib (provided through the Office of the Treaty Commissioner) is gratefully acknowledged in the preparation of this publication. We thank as well Maisie Cardinal and Raymond Cardinal for the assistance they provided in the preparation and completion of this text.

Finally, we wish to acknowledge the untiring support and co-operation received from the Office of the Treaty Commissioner. If it had not been for the persistence and unflagging support of Treaty Commissioner David Arnot, Kay Lerat, and Nicole Jule, this book would not have been possible.

Harold Cardinal
Walter Hildebrandt

Context

At the beginning of the Federation of Saskatchewan Indian Nations' Treaty Elders Forums, Elder Jimmy Myo told us:

> You cannot begin to understand the treaties unless you understand our cultural and spiritual traditions and our Indian laws.[1]

Treaty 6 Elder Peter Waskahat said:

> The non-Indian has to become aware of both the fundamentals and the depth of our way of worship because our inner soul is connected to Creation.[2]

Accordingly, in this publication of the Saskatchewan Elders' presentations, we commence with a discussion of those spiritual foundations. The Elders wanted us to focus our effort at seeking an Indian understanding of treaties on the spiritual foundations underlying the treaty-making process. We wish to note at the outset that some of the Elders, in their traditional diplomatic manner, gently, but clearly, reminded us that in seeking such an understanding, it was necessary to observe both the traditional processes and forms required by First Nations spiritual laws.

The treaties cannot be understood in isolation. Non-Aboriginal understanding of treaties and the treaty process is shaped by its colonial history. The First Nations' perspective must be understood in the context of their world views. The Elders made it clear that, in their view, those who seek to understand Indian treaties must become aware of the significance of First Nations spiritual traditions, beliefs, and ceremonies underlying the treaty-making process. Each meeting with Elders opened and closed with either prayer or drum or pipe ceremonies. Each meeting was conducted mainly in the Elders' First Nations languages.

Treaty 6 Elder Norman Sunchild said:

> Our ancestors spent their lifetime studying, meditating, and living the way of life required to understand those traditions, teachings, and laws in which the treaties are rooted. In their study, they rooted their physical and spiritual beings directly on Mother Earth as a way of establishing a connectedness to the Creator and His Creation. Through that connectedness, they received the conceptual knowledge they required and the capacity to verbalize and describe the many blessings bestowed on them by the Creator. They were meticulous in following the disciplines, processes, and procedures required for such an endeavour.[3]

If we are to reach an understanding of the treaties that are rooted in these traditions, we, likewise, must pay close attention to the discipline, processes, and procedures.

Elder Jimmy Myo, Moosomin First Nation, Treaty 6; Photo: © Marian Dinwoodie

Elder Norman Sunchild, Thunderchild First Nation, Treaty 6

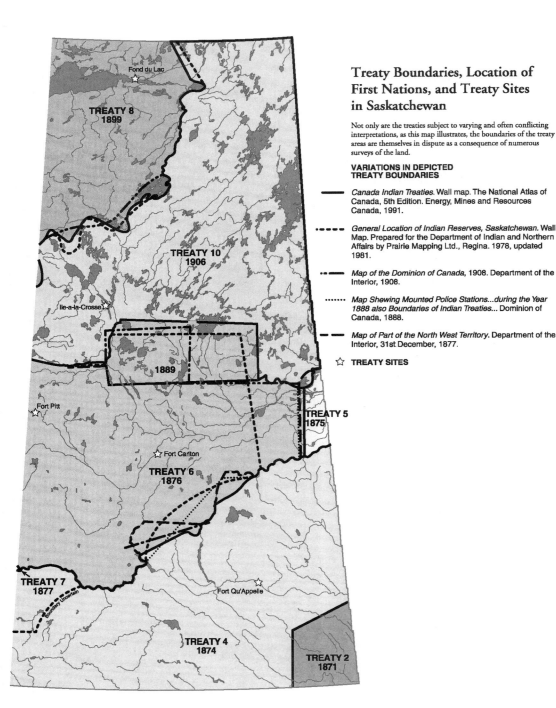

Treaty Boundaries, Location of First Nations, and Treaty Sites in Saskatchewan

Not only are the treaties subject to varying and often conflicting interpretations, as this map illustrates, the boundaries of the treaty areas are themselves in dispute as a consequence of numerous surveys of the land.

VARIATIONS IN DEPICTED TREATY BOUNDARIES

——— *Canada Indian Treaties.* Wall map. The National Atlas of Canada, 5th Edition. Energy, Mines and Resources Canada, 1991.

– – – *General Location of Indian Reserves, Saskatchewan.* Wall Map. Prepared for the Department of Indian and Northern Affairs by Prairie Mapping Ltd., Regina. 1978, updated 1981.

–·–·– *Map of the Dominion of Canada,* 1908. Department of the Interior, 1908.

·········· *Map Shewing Mounted Police Stations...during the Year 1888 also Boundaries of Indian Treaties...* Dominion of Canada, 1888.

– – *Map of Part of the North West Territory.* Department of the Interior, 31st December, 1877.

☆ **TREATY SITES**

The attitude and preparation required by individuals seeking spiritual knowledge was described by Elder Kay Thompson as follows:

> Seeking knowledge about our ways requires we approach those things in a clean way. In our ways, cleanliness of the mind and body could be achieved only by the selection of a clean place away from human habitation where sweat lodges, ceremonies, fasts, and quiet meditation could be carried out.[4]

The Elders' comments allude to formal and long-established ways, procedures, and processes that First Nations persons are required to follow when seeking particular kinds of knowledge that are rooted in spiritual traditions and laws. The rules that are applied to this way of learning are strict, and the seekers of knowledge are required to follow meticulous procedures and processes as they prepare for and enter the "quest for knowledge journey."

Some Elders describe this as the "formal education system" of First Nations. It is a way of learning that is culturally integral to the transmission of knowledge through First Nations oral and spiritual traditions. These requirements need to be carefully integrated in any ongoing treaty process that seeks to derive an Indian understanding of treaty.

The Starting Point for Treaty Discussions

Enduring White Images of Indians:

> Indian peoples were found scattered wide-cast over the continent, having as a characteristic, no fixed abodes, but moving as the exigencies of living demanded. As *heathens and barbarians* it was not thought that they had any proprietary title to the soil [*emphasis added*].
> *Regina* v. *St. Catherine's Milling* (1885)[5]

> ... and there is no doubt, to quote Hobbes, that aboriginal life in the territory was, at best "nasty, brutish and short."
> *Delgamuukw* v. *B.C.*[6]

> The origins of the Gistskan and Wet' Suet'in and other aboriginal peoples in the northwest part of the province are unknown. It is generally believed they immigrated here from Asia.
> *Delgamuukw* v. *B.C.*[7]

Much of Canadian history pertaining to First Nations depicts them as "heathen, savage, primitive peoples." For many in Canada, Canadian history begins with the arrival of Europeans to North America in general and to Canada in particular.

First Nations Perspectives:

The Elders begin by locating the history of their nations in North America in a time continuum stretching thousands of years, starting with the beginning of time itself. The Elders view the treaties as part of that First Nations historical continuum.

In the teachings that were passed on to them, First Nations' histories begin with the creation and the placement of First Nations peoples on the North American continent by the Creator. They were placed in North America as "children of the Creator" (*otawâsimisimâwak*). In their view, as "children of the Creator," their peoples, like others, were endowed with a mind or intellect (*mâmitonêyihcikan*) along with all their other faculties, for the Creator in his perfect goodness wanted them to understand the fullness and completeness of His blessings (*sawêyihtâkosiwin*).

Creation, in the eyes of the Elders, is followed by a history measured in thousands of years during which time, like many other peoples or nations, First Nations evolved and grew within the spiritual traditions given to them by the Creator and, in the process, developed their political, social, educational, economic, and spiritual structures and institutions. As First Nations societies developed over time, they evolved their respective relationships to the lands given to them by the Creator.

Elder Gordon Oakes stated that it is important for non-First Nations peoples to

Chief Poundmaker (1840-1886) and his fourth wife. A vocal critic of the federal government, he was convicted of treason and was sent to prison in November 1885. Saskatchewan Archives Board

© *Tourism Saskatchewan*

understand that, for First Nations, the beginning point is Creation and the placement of First Nations by the Creator on the lands found in North America.

Treaty 6 Elder Jacob Bill stated:

> The word "*nistamêyimâkan*" means "the first born or the ones who first received our ways" – ways that we use to communicate with our Creator and His Creation. The Creator conceived the First Nations on this island [North America] – the nations that were first created here were given a way to pray. The very first people who were here were very strong. Their prayers were very strong because of the way they were taught to pray – it is clear in their minds because they were the first generation when life began. So when a person is praying ... he thinks about the first generation of First Nations ... there he has a sense of identity and recognition and prays to them for help.... We remember the first born in our prayers because he was the one who first received the blessing from the Creator. That is what the word "*nistamêyimâkan*" means.[8]

Treaty 4 Saulteaux Elder Dolly Neapetung remarked:

> The Creator gave us a way of life and a language by which we could speak to one another and speak to Him and give meaning to everything that was around us, to help us understand the world and other people, our relatives.... God gave us this land. We own it as people, as a nation.[9]

Elder Bart McDonald from the Denesuline Nation said:

> Let's remember the Creator who created all these things, all the resources, why he created everything for us.[10]

One of the Dene leaders, Acting Chief Victor Echodh explained:

> And as you know we, the Dene here, we were put here by the Creator on this earth to live with a certain purpose, with a certain way, we know that; we see that in our ways, our land, wildlife that provides for us. In terms of written document[s] and documentation of our ways, we weren't given the opportunity to do that, how the Creator put us on this Earth is basically how we continue to live today. We exercise it every day, what the land provides for us, and our people are healthy as a result of it. The land is healthy as a result of what the Creator does for it. Rain, snow, winter, summer ... the seasons of the year, all keep everything in balance and we as people live in balance with those seasons. We go from one season to the next. That's how we lived before the White man came here, we shared, we worked with each other.[11]

The Elders of the Dene, Cree, Assiniboine, and Saulteaux peoples presented remarkably similar and consistent descriptions of their belief systems, in spite of the fact that they come from widely divergent regions, speak different languages, and each practise their own distinct cultural traditions.

The Elders explain that the Creator made North America as a place where the spiritual traditions and teachings required that First Nations follow a way of life predicated upon peace and harmony.

The Elders are careful to fully acknowledge the life-giving power of Creation as evidenced in the natural forces that surround them. They describe the care and sensitivity with which First

Elder Jacob Bill, Pelican Lake First Nation, Treaty 6

Elder Kay Thompson, Carry the Kettle First Nation, Treaty 4

Acting Chief Victor Echodh, Black Lake Denesuline Nation, Treaty 8

Chief Pasquah, c. 1895. He argued that the land belonged to the Indians and that the £300,000 paid to the Hudson's Bay Company should have been given to them. The Presbyterian Archives in Canada Graphics Collection

Nations ways evolved to reflect the respect that must be accorded to the Creator, and all his Creation, and the way in which these traditions are held sacred by their people.

Elder Peter Waskahat told us:

> On this land, in the past and even today we were very careful about what we were given – what we were given through the uses of everything on the land, Creation. We were very careful, we had our own teachings, our own education system – teaching children that way of life was taught [by] the grandparents and extended families; they were taught how to view and respect the land and everything in Creation. Through that the young people were taught how to live, what the Creator's laws were, what were the natural laws, what were these First Nations' laws ... the teachings revolved around a way of life that was based on their values.[12]

Treaty 4 Assiniboine Elder Kay Thompson stated:

> Due to the pipe, there was a lot of respect amongst the Indians long ago ... they would go to a sweat to purify themselves and pray in there through the pipe and then they [would] go and fast on a hill, the highest hill they could find.... They would fast and pray out there, and they prayed for everything, for the knowledge they had. They prayed with the roots they had for healing. They had to fast and pray until they got their answer from the Great Spirit.... [T]hey communicated through visions, through dreams, that's how they got their answer from the Creator.[13]

Victor Echodh, Acting Chief of the Black Lake Denesuline Nation, said:

> That is how we lived before the White man came here, we shared, we worked with each other ... we basically have developed ways of working with each other and sharing with each other, we respect the land, we respect the wildlife, we respect each other.[14]

Saulteaux Elder Dolly Neapetung of Treaty 4 told us:

> The Creator put these [wildlife, medicines, plants] here and put us here. The Creator gave us this land. I still ... live and try to live in the old ways and the ways of our traditional living, the ways that our old people lived. We were taught to care for our old people, we were taught to respect them, we were taught to listen to their stories because their stories spoke of life.[15]

For the Saskatchewan Elders, the treaties negotiated by their nations with the British Crown after 1874 arose from the teachings and prophecies arising from their spiritual traditions. Their analysis of the treaties is centred upon the framework of their spiritual traditions.

Hence, when the Elders talk about treaties, they begin with a theoretical perspective dictated by the spiritual foundations and processes upon which the First Nations negotiated the treaties. They describe the spiritual principles, traditions, protocols, and ceremonies used by the First Nations treaty makers to explain the objectives that First Nations sought to achieve in the treaty-making processes that they entered into.

They emphasized that the First Nations' first and foremost objective in the treaty-making process was to have the new peoples arriving in their territories recognize and affirm their continuing right to maintain, as peoples, the First Nations relationships with the Creator through the laws given to them by Him. The Elders explained that the laws First Nations follow are given to them by the Creator and firmly emphasized their belief that the starting point of discussions on treaties is their relationship to the Creator.

In the First Nations history passed on to the Elders, the arrival of the Europeans to the North American continent and the subsequent treaty relationship negotiated with them were reflected as part of First Nations teachings, which had foretold the arrival of the Europeans to North America. These First Nations teachings identified for First Nations the framework upon which they were to create relationships with the arriving Europeans. First Nations traditions and teachings required that the relationships they created with the Europeans be governed by the laws, values, and principles that First Nations had received from the Creator. These laws and principles described the relationships and responsibilities they possessed to and for the lands given to them by the Creator.

In the treaty negotiations, both the First Nations and British negotiators accorded a prominent role to persons responsible for institutions representing the spiritual traditions of each of the treaty parties.

Elders refer to the spiritual ceremonies conducted and spiritual symbols used by First Nations and the active participation of various Christian missionaries along with the Christian symbols utilized by the Crown in those negotiations to assert that both parties anchored their goals and objectives on the values and principles contained in the teachings of each of their own spiritual traditions.

In the view of the Elders, the treaty nations – First Nations and the Crown – solemnly promised the Creator that they would conduct their relationships with each other in accordance with the laws, values, and principles given to each of them by the Creator.

Treaty 6 Elder Norman Sunchild stated:

> When [Treaty 6 First Nations] finally agreed to the treaty, the Commissioner took the promises in his hand and raised them to the skies, placing the treaties in the hands of the Great Spirit.[16]

Elder Jacob Bill of Treaty 6 also commented:

> It was the will of the Creator that the White man would come here to live with us, among us, to share our lives together with him, and also both of us collectively to benefit from the bounty of Mother Earth for all time to come.[17]

The duties and obligations that arise from the laws, ceremonies, and traditions that form a way of life for the First Nations are clear. The Elders, for example, explained that when promises, agreements, or vows are formally made to the Creator (*wiyôhtâwîmâw*) through ceremonies conducted in accordance with the laws governing them – the promises, agreements, or vows so made are irrevocable and inviolable.

Breaking these vows can bring about divine retribution with grave consequences. This concept is known in Cree as "*pâstâhowin.*" The Elders discussed this concept wondering if the

Cree/Sauteaux Chief Moosomin. He agreed to Treaty 6 in 1879 and had a reputation for being a pacifist. Moosomin is reported to have draped a Union Jack over his shoulders to show that he and his band had no sympathy with the Riel Rebellion. Saskatchewan Archives Board

Elder Lawrence Tobacco, Kawacatoose First Nation, Treaty 4

Left to right: Charlie Throassie (Black Lake First Nation), Pat Robillard (Black Lake First Nation), Leon Fern (Fond du Lac First Nation), Pauline Mercredi (Fond du Lac First Nation), Agnes Alphonse (Black Lake First Nation), and Angus Tsannie (Hatchet Lake First Nation).

White man understood the consequences that can flow when human beings unleash the wrath of the Creator by breaching fundamental responsibilities to Him.

Elder Jacob Bill remarked:

> I wonder if the White man understands that. Me and my friend ... were thinking that maybe it is time that [the White man] should know and we should tell him. Maybe that will straighten him, if he understands how dangerous it is to breach sacred undertakings.[18]

Treaty 6 Elder Jimmy Myo commented:

> We have laws as Indian people and those laws are not man-made, they were given to us by God.... But in my law, if you do such a thing [breach a sacred undertaking], even if no other human being is aware of it, you will always carry that for the rest of your life. Some part of it here on earth, you will pay for it, something might happen, you might lose something that is more important than what you stole.... If you lie, it is the same thing ... you will carry that. It will always be with you. And when you die, that is when you really pay for it. That is what the law says; our law says that the amount we do not pay here on earth, when we die will pay for it.[19]

Treaty 6 Elder Jacob Bill further remarked:

> This is what our Elders have told us. We pay attention to what those Elders had to say because in the past they were given certain powerful things, they were guided by traditions and ways of worship given to us by the Creator – they were spiritual and powerful Elders who were able to provide prophecies as to what would happen in the future ... they were advised to uphold the treaties ... they told us that it was very dangerous to breach treaties ... that something will happen – if either of the treaty signatory nations breach the treaties ... we do not want to see the treaties breached ... the consequences of incurring the wrath of the Creator will be punishment similar to that which accompanies the use of a big whip.[20]

Elder Lawrence Tobacco gave the following descriptions:

> ...what I have said, the sun, the river, and the grass, I have mentioned them; spirits for each one of them. If I don't deal with them, I could get punished too. My ancestors have set it up for me to deal with them in a proper way. That's what I'm trying to do. I'm not fooling around with the treaties.[21]

For the Elders, both the discussion and implementation of the treaties must be approached with respect, care, and sensitivity.

Shared First Nations Foundations

The Cree, Dene, Assiniboine, and Saulteaux Nations, who negotiated the treaties found in what is now known as Saskatchewan, share spiritual philosophies, teachings, laws, and traditions that are remarkably similar to one another. There is an interconnectedness (*ê-miciminitômakahki*) among the sacred ceremonies, teachings, and beliefs of First Nations. Each of the treaty First Nations possesses its own unique language and cultural traditions. Yet in spite of that, the Elders are able in their discussions with one another to identify a unique First Nations world view and philosophy.

Treaty Elders expressed their unease with any treaty process that is divided on a region-specific or First Nations-specific basis because such an approach does not accord with the fundamentally unified First Nations spiritual philosophies and teachings that accompanied the treaty negotiations in Saskatchewan.

This point was remarkably evident throughout the many discussions held with the Elders who presented descriptions of Cree, Assiniboine, Saulteaux, and Dene teachings and belief systems that were similar and consistent with each other. Particularly among the Cree, Assiniboine, and Saulteaux Nations, the Elders pointed to the inter-nation aspect of their spiritual traditions, which enables individuals from their respective nations to actively participate in different traditional ceremonies conducted by the different treaty nations.

Elder Peter Waskahat of the Frog Lake First Nation said:

> We are all one voice. That is why I go from treaty to treaty asking that question and also sharing my teachings of treaty.[22]

Elder Norman Sunchild of the Thunderchild First Nation stated that:

> Our Elders of the past understood this history, it was not to be changed, and there should be one account of treaty history.... Today you see many things are being controlled for us. This should never have happened, it should have been followed as the Elders have said in the way that the treaties were concluded.[23]

Some suggested that a preferable approach to seeking an Indian understanding of the treaties would be to bring all the treaty Elders from the different treaty areas together under one process.

Treaty 8 Elders unveil a commemoration plaque at the 100th anniversary of Treaty 8 at Fond du Lac.

Iyiniw sawêyihtâkosiwin
The Peoples' Sacred Gifts

© Tourism Saskatchewan

In the Cree language, the word *"iyiniwak"* means the "peoples." It is a word that is used by Cree speakers to describe all First Nations peoples in North America.

The Cree words *"iyiniw miyikowisowina"* (that which has been given to the peoples) and *"iyiniw sawêyihtâkosiwin"* (the peoples' sacred gifts) are used to describe those special gifts that originate in the special relationship that First Nations peoples have with the Creator and the blessings or gifts that devolve to the peoples collectively and individually from that relationship.

The traditional teachings of the First Nations in Saskatchewan tell them that they are the children of the Creator. It was the Creator who put them on Mother Earth. For this reason, the Cree refer to North America as *"iyiniwi-ministik"* (the Peoples' Island).

First Nations Elders say they have been on this land from time immemorial. They say, with all that the Creator gave them, they were and are fortunate peoples, rich in terms of the quality, beauty, and content of the lands given to them. They were spiritually enriched living amidst the great natural endowment of the Creator. The Elders relate how they were given animals for food and shelter, water to drink and to make things grow, trees for shelter, fuel and ceremonies, plants for medicines, rocks to help make fire and for arrowheads. The First Peoples had everything they needed in the world around them. The Creator gave them all that they needed to survive both spiritually and materially.

The Elders emphasize the sacredness of the Earth, and in particular the sacredness of the Peoples' Island – North America – that was given to their peoples to live on. The Elders say that the Creator gave the First Nations peoples the lands in North America. The Elders maintain that the land belongs to their peoples as their peoples belong to the land. The land, waters, and all life-giving forces in North America were, and are, an integral part of a sacred relationship with the Creator. The land and water could never be sold or given away by their Nations. For that reason, the Elders say that the sacred Earth given to the First Nations by the Creator will always be theirs. But more than land was given by the Creator.

"Iyiniw miyikowisowina" (that which has been given to the peoples) and *"iyiniw sawêyihtâkosiwin"* (the peoples' sacred gifts) are generic terms that are used to describe gifts deriving from the peoples' special relationship with the Creator, whether those gifts are material in nature (land) or metaphysical (as in the case of laws, values, principles, and mores that guide or regulate the peoples' conduct in

all their many and varied relationships). The Elders are emphatic in their belief that it is this very special and complete relationship with the Creator that is the source of the sovereignty that their peoples possess. It provided the framework for the political, social, educational, and cultural institutions and laws of their peoples that allowed them to survive as nations from the beginning of time to the present. In their view, it is part of the divine birthright given to their peoples by the Creator.

The elements of that thinking are reflected in the following statement by Elder Peter Waskahat of the Frog Lake First Nation:

> A livelihood, that was taught, that was what we had; it revolved around survival of the people, and a lot of this livelihood was taught from the teachings of many generations, the teachings from Creation; that is how they saw their world. For example, we had our own doctors, our own medicine people. There was a lot of teachings, lifelong teachings that were passed from generation to generation ... so we had our own medical system as well, we had our own leaders and those leaders had the teachings.[24]

All the things that First Nations required for survival were given to them by the Creator, whether reflected by the life-giving and life-sustaining forces represented by sun, water, grass, animals, fire, or Mother Earth. These blessings were all they needed for their survival and the development of North America.

Elder Isabel McNab from Treaty 4 remarked:

> Like I said, the Indian people prior to treaty-making were not savages. They never

were and they never will be. Because they knew God, they worshipped God and they worshiped His Creations, thanked Him for the things that God gave them. And it was told to me by my Grandfather, Old Gambler [who is mentioned in the treaty negotiations], he said ... that these old people were gathering and having a ceremony, spiritual ceremony and they had told their people that they had to prepare

Fort Smith, Treaty Proceedings, 1898. Provincial Archives of Manitoba

Elder Isabel McNab,
Gordon First Nation,
Treaty 4

Elder Frank McIntyre,
English River
Denesuline Nation,
Treaty 10; Photo:
© Marian Dinwoodie

themselves, they had to prepare for something great that was going to happen. And they were told by the Elders, he said, "there's a stranger coming from across these waters that's going to come and take the land away from you, if you are not ready. And only God can do those things. It can't be anything else, it can't be a stone or whatever. God chose to talk to the Indian people like that and prepare them. So the Indian people were always fearful and knew God and worshipped God in their own way. And they prepared themselves.[25]

The Elders told us that the First Nations relied on the spiritual and psychological strength they received from the various life-giving, life-sustaining forces reflected in the diverse elements of Creation. These elements are represented by the Creator's other children – the spirit community that surrounded them, such as those of the eagle, the buffalo, the wind, the thunder, and the trees.

Elder Jacob Bill of the Pelican Lake First Nation said:

> The indigenous person was given a lot by the Creator through the grandfathers ... the spirit grandfathers who are accountable to the Creator. The spirit, in giving a vision and advice to the human spirit ... was disseminated through a ritual. And ... translating that vision had to be the ultimate truth.[26]

In spite of the different cultural backgrounds of the peoples of Saskatchewan, the purposes of First Nations ceremonies are similar. In the ceremonial world of the prairie First Nations, sweetgrass, fire, the pipe, and tobacco served as the primary connection between the First Nations and their Creator and His Creation.

For the Dene, the ceremonial fires form an integral and necessary element of their feasts, as do their drums, tobacco, and other rich spiritual traditions. At the core, the elements used by the Dene function in the same way as those used in the traditions of the prairie First Nations – they serve as the connectors or the medium through which the peoples communicate with and relate to the Creator and His Creation.

Multilingual Elder Frank McIntyre of the English River Denesuline Nation stated:

> My father used to tell me, we need to make a thanksgiving ... [he said,] you know my son, we are alone and you may think we are the first persons in this area, but our great-grandfathers were here before us.... I am going to sing to bring a thanksgiving to the Creator and to Mother Earth who has supplied us. Now, you sing with me if you can. So he starts singing and I start repeating his song with him and he would tell me to stop. So we would stop, now listen to our grandfathers and great-grandfathers. You can hear them singing with us. In every hill around us you could hear the echo, even further, now you hear that? We are not the first persons in this country. They were our forefathers, our great-grandfathers that were here. I could hear all the echo around us and that the spirit of our great grandfathers and also that is the Mother Earth supporting us.[27]

Elders at Waterhen Lake, July 1998

Miyo-wîcêhtowin
The Principle of Getting Along Well with Others, Good Relations, Expanding the Circle

Chief Carry the Kettle, Treaty 4, with an unidentified man, Assiniboine, 1910. Morris Collection, Provincial Archives of Manitoba

"*Miyo-wîcêhtowin*" is a Cree word meaning "having or possessing good relations." It is a concept that arises from one of the core doctrines or values of the Cree Nation. The term outlines the nature of the relationships that Cree peoples are required to establish. It asks, directs, admonishes, or requires Cree peoples as individuals and as a nation to conduct themselves in a manner such that they create positive or good relations in all relationships, be it individually or collectively with other peoples. "*Miyo-wîcêhtowin*" as a concept and as a term originates in the laws and relationships that their nation has with the Creator.

The doctrine of "good relations" is an essential and integral component of the teachings of all the Treaty First Nations in Saskatchewan. It is perhaps best symbolized by the circle evident in the way many First Nations ceremonies are structured.

The circle has come to be recognized as occupying an important symbolic role among First Nations. Elders Gordon Oakes, Jimmy Myo, and Jacob Bill tell us that it is not without good reason that it has acquired such recognition. They told us that, in a ceremonial setting such as the Sundance, which is the most sacred and important ceremony of the prairie tribes, the circular structure of both the ceremonial lodge and the encampment surrounding the lodge serves as an affirmation of the unity between First Nations' political and social organizations with their Creator, and their spiritual institutions – an affirmation not possible without the essential element of *miyo-wîcêhtowin*.

The Elders stated that the circle symbolized the oneness of First Nations people with the Creator and the spiritual, social, and political institutions of the First Nations. It is at once a statement of allegiance, of loyalty, fidelity, and unity by both the nation and its peoples. This act/statement is rooted in the doctrine of *wâhkôhtowin* (the laws governing all relations) and *miyo-wîcêhtowin* (the laws concerning good relations).

In this particular context, the Elders told us that the circle represents a coming together or a bringing together of a nation. They state that, in coming together in this manner, the nation reaffirms its unity under the laws of the Creator. Under First Nations' traditional teaching, this was one of the sacred ways in which the nation would continue to possess the capability to nurture, protect, care for, and heal its people. It is these annual acts of renewal and spiritual and community refurbishment that enabled the Treaty First Nations to retain their inner strength, cohesion, and spiritual integrity.

The Elders stated that it is for such reasons that the circle has come to be known variously as – a praying circle, talking circle, healing circle, and a circle of reconciliation. The circle, in this context, represented a coming together or a bringing together of a community or a nation. For the Elders, a nation united under the laws of the Creator represents a healthy, strong, and stable nation, possessing the capability to nurture, protect, and care for and heal its people.

Powerful laws were established to protect and to nurture the foundations of strong, vibrant nations. Foremost amongst these laws are those related to human bonds and relationships known as the laws relating to *miyo-wîcêhtowin*. The laws of *miyo-wîcêhtowin* include those laws encircling the bonds of human relationships in the ways in which they are created, nourished, reaffirmed, and recreated as a means of strengthening the unity among First Nations people and of the nation itself. For First Nations, these are integral and indispensable components of their way of life. These teachings constitute the essential elements underlying the First Nations notions of peace, harmony, and good relations, which must be maintained as required by the Creator. The teachings and ceremonies are the means given to First Nations to restore peace and harmony in times of personal and community conflict. These teachings also serve as the foundation upon which new relationships are to be created.

For Treaty First Nations, these sacred laws or doctrines constitute indispensable components of the treaties entered into with the British Crown in the latter part of the 1800s. For the Elders, the relationships created by treaties were founded upon the doctrines of *wâhkôhtowin* and *miyo-wîcêhtowin* for they constituted the essential elements of an enduring and lasting relationship between the First Nations, the Crown, and her subjects. These relationships were, in part, to consist of mutual ongoing caring and sharing arrangements between the treaty parties, which included a sharing of the duties and responsibilities for land, shared for livelihood purposes with the newcomers.

To understand the depth of the Elders' beliefs, we must provide a brief outline and description of some of these beliefs. There is great depth and complexity of meaning attached to the ceremonies and teachings of First Nations. Elders and spiritual leaders are careful not to unduly share all their sacred information and practices, but they are willing to share sufficient material to allow non-Aboriginal people to better understand First Nations' world view and the spiritual foundation of the treaties.

Elder Peter Waskahat commented:

> When you look at First Nation's people on this land, in the past, even today, we are careful about what we were given to do. We were given the uses of everything on the land and Creation. We had ... our own teachings, our own education system teaching children that way of life, and how children were taught how to view, to respect the land and everything in Creation. Through that, the young people were [educated about] what were the Creator's laws, what were these natural laws. What

Chief J.B. George, English River First Nation, 1935. Saskatchewan Archives Board

Elder Gordon Oakes,
Nekaneet First Nation,
Treaty 4

were these First Nations laws. And talk revolved around a way of life based on these values. For example: respect, to share, to care, to be respectful of people, how to help oneself. How to help others. How to work together....

And when the other people came, all other First Nations know of these teachings of this traditional education system. Everyone had a role. Hunters, the Elders, grandmothers. Even looking for food, there were teachings for the young, for the adults,

for the grandparents. A livelihood that was taught, that was what they had ... survival of a people. In a lot of this, livelihood was taught ... [to] many generations teaching from Creation. That is how they saw their world and understood their world. For example, [we] Indians had our own doctors, our own medicine people.

[There are] a lot of teachings. Lifelong teachings that were passed on from generation to generation. They know sicknesses, they know the plants, and they knew how to treat our people of certain sicknesses. So we had our own system as well. We had our own leadership ... very highly respected for a chance to lead their people. So we had all those things.

We had our own First Nations' government; we had our own life teachings on education. Even when a person had made mistakes in life, there were people that would counsel them. There was a process of reconciliation. It was done through the oral language. It was done through the Elders. There they talked about that person getting back into a balanced life and were made aware of how [to] focus [on] what was important in life.

And if that person had listened and took the appropriate guidance from those kinds of people and they would get back into a balance and be able to help them, to learn from these things. To become a part of the family, part of their nations.

That is how we/they looked at life. That's the Indian way of life, and all First Nations people had understandings of different customs, different traditions ... that was their life.[28]

© Tourism Saskatchewan

Beardy's and Okemasis Pow Wow

© *Ted Whitecalf*

Wiyôhtâwîmâw
The Divine Father

Chiefs Conference at Thunderchild Reserve, 1922. Several Chiefs are shown wearing their Treaty medals. Saskatchewan Archives Board

In the Cree language, the Creator is referred to in many ways, but one of the most common references is "*wiyôhtâwîmâw*" (the Father).

One of the most enduring stereotypes of First Nations peoples is the general perception that Indians did not know of the existence of God before the coming of Europeans to the Americas. Treaty Commissioner Alexander Morris once advised:

> Let us have Christianity and civilization
> to leaven the mass of heathenism and
> paganism among the Indian tribes.[29]

While this view has more recently been tempered by the acknowledgement by some of the Christian denominations (who were responsible in large part for creating the stereotype) that the characterization was wrong, the perception still endures.

The Elders, for that reason, were adamant about the continuing need to correct the false historical assumptions and the depictions of Indians as savages who did not know God or who did not possess any spiritual traditions or laws. Though they appreciated the statements of reconciliation issued on this matter by both the Canadian government and some of the Christian churches, they insisted that there is continuing need for First Nations to explain their beliefs of the Father and the relationship of those beliefs to the treaty process.

The spiritual traditions of the First Nations are based first and foremost on the belief that there is only one God, often referred to as the Father or Creator.[30]

Dene Elder Pauline Mercredi commented:

> Our Creator who is in heaven, helps us, the
> children; he has given every one of us a life.
> We all came from the Creator, Dene people,
> the White people, all the different tribes; we
> do have one Creator. And let's work together
> because of that. We should encourage one
> another and respect our way of life.[31]

The First Nations believe that the relationship is governed by divine laws that define the relations between the Creator and what He created. The relationship between the Creator and First Nations peoples is understood to be like that which exists between the various members of a family and is thus governed by laws of *wâhkôhtowin*, laws detailing the duties and responsibilities which take effect for each member of the family unit.

The First Nations concept of family is seen as the organizing conceptual framework through which the relationships created by treaty are to be understood. The laws governing *wâhkôhtowin* are applied by analogy to various elements of the treaty relationship.

From a traditional perspective, the global application of the family analogy to relations between nations originates from the First Nations notion that the Creator is the creator and father (*wiyôhtâwîmâw*) of all peoples and all of Creation. Traditional teachings state that the Creator created different peoples and placed them on different lands all around the world.

During our Treaty Elders Forum at Fond du Lac, an Elder remarked:

> We were all related, interrelated, and supposed to respect and love one another. We are not the authority, the ultimate authority. The ultimate authority is the Creator.[32]

An Elder from the Gordon's First Nation, Isabel McNab, said:

> [The] God that we serve is greater than all the governments that are in Ottawa. And He was the One that was holding hands with Indian people. And He's the One that prepares the way for us.[33]

Saulteaux Elder Dolly Neapetung spoke of the Creator in this way:

> The Creator ... gave us a way to worship and then talked about the day when the foreigners would come and the people that have come here ... to borrow the land. That we did not in any way at all, ever give it up ... we don't as one individual among ourselves own the land.[34]

Treaty 4 Assiniboine Elder Kay Thompson commented:

Cree Chiefs meeting with Edgar Dewdney, 1885. Glenbow Archives

Elder Pauline Mercredi, Fond du Lac Denesuline Nation, Treaty 8

Elder Dolly Neapetung, Yellow Quill First Nation, Treaty 4

Elder Alma Kytwayhat, Makwa Sahgaiehcan First Nation, Treaty 6

Nakoda law, Nakoda philosophy, Nakoda way of life organizes itself around the concept of *Metah Koyabi* [which] means "all my relations." We are tied to all our relations. That's everything. We are all part of the Creator. This relationship is *Ade Wakan Tunga* and is respected through the pipe.[35]

According to the Elders, the many ceremonies that First Nations were given came as a gift from the Father to enable First Nations peoples to maintain a continuing relationship with the Father and His Creation. Part of those gifts required that First Nations peoples maintain a connectedness to Mother Earth and all of her life-sustaining forces.

The Elders understood that, through the treaties, the British Crown undertook to respect the "way of life" of the First Nations and not interfere with their belief systems. The most blatant breaches of the Crown's treaty undertakings relating to the freedom of association and freedom of movement have long been removed from Canadian statutes. However, other laws have come into being that continue to interfere with the treaty undertaking.

In relation to access to particular plants for ceremonial and medicinal purposes, Treaty 6 Elder Alma Kytwayhat said:

We are told that these treaties were to last forever. The government and the government officials, the Commissioner, told us that, as long as the grass grows, and the sun rises from the east and sets in the west, and the river flows, these treaties will last. We were given rights, yet now we can't enjoy them.

We were given the right to also gather our medicines and go out into those gathering lands as we have always done in our traditional times. And take them so that we can heal one another and take care of one another as the old people did and taught us to.

But we can't do that now. We can't do these things because the government has again broken that. We now have to get permission.... I understand that our young people and our people now have to get permits to go and gather our traditional foods that were there, given to us by the Creator. They were promised to us under treaty – we would never lose. They have again broken this.[36]

The Elders believe that a better understanding of the relationship that First Nations have with the Creator would result in greater respect from non-Aboriginal people, and they believe that this understanding could be a starting point for the healing that many communities need to undergo.

Miskâsowin

Finding One's Sense of Origin and Belonging, Finding "One's Self" or Finding "One's Centre"

The White man's Colonial Mission Statement:

> Now it is evident from the history of "the reserves," that the Indians there are regarded no longer as in a wild and primitive state, but as in a condition of transition from barbarism to civilization. The object of the system is to segregate the red from the white population, in order that the former may be trained up to a level with the latter. *Regina v. St. Catherines Milling Co.*[37]

The centuries-old assimilation projects of Canada aimed at "civilizing" the Indian were predicated on the belief that a sense of shame (shame about being an Indian) should be inculcated in the minds, souls, and hearts of First Nations children. Generation upon generation of First Nations children were forcibly removed from their homes and brought into "educational institutions" where, among other things, they were programmed to abhor anything that contained, reflected, or symbolized their First Nations heritage.

Some of the Elders who made presentations at the Treaty Elders Forums gave heart-rending accounts of the painful and horrid experiences that they encountered and the anguish they felt then and still continue to feel as a consequence of those state-sponsored experiments. The presentations were difficult both for the Elders and for those who listened – for such was the pain being expressed that even the most hardened of heart would have been moved to tears.

For some people, these state-sponsored experiments have played havoc on their families, literally tearing them apart at the seams. Government policies even dictated who could be treaty and who could not be treaty. Alfred Billette from the Buffalo River Denesuline Nation recounts how his family was torn apart:

Alfred Billette, Buffalo River Denesuline Nation, Treaty 10

> In my family, some of our relatives are treaty, others are Métis and some are non-status. This happened when my father was young. He became treaty and took the name "Billette." Another brother became Métis and took the last name "Cummings" and the third brother "Lemaigre" and a sister who married a Mongrand also was not recognized as treaty because of that too. This problem is also prevalent on my mother's side too, after my dad died she married a non-Dene and lost her rights. This is creating a rift between family members. We know we're Dene but we don't know what status we are. We need to resolve this matter immediately.[38]

For many of the Elders, though those state-sponsored experiments have been discontinued, the negative stereotyping of First Nations peoples continues to find public expression.

Chief Jacob Johnstone, Mistawasis, Saskatchewan.
Saskatchewan Archives Board

Some of the Elders who made presentations expressed an increasing concern with what appears to be a well-coordinated and well-planned public effort by some to resurrect and re-legitimize racist stereotypical images of First Nations and their people.

Some of the Elders, particularly the grandmothers, made impassioned presentations describing the devastating cumulative effects that they were witnessing at the grassroots level, which both the negative stereotyping of First Nations peoples and the state-sponsored experiments continue to cause. They described how they, their communities, and families were continuing to suffer. They described both the trauma and destruction they were witnessing among too many First Nations peoples.

The grandmothers pointed to the number of First Nations peoples who are in jails, the number who have become dependent upon alcohol and drugs, the number who are increasingly found in the streets, the rising number of suicides, and the many other ways in which First Nations communities continue to be traumatized.

Many of the Elders who made presentations pointed out that repairing the treaty relationship with the Crown, bringing healing to First Nations, and bringing about good relations (*miyo-wîcêhtowin*) between and among the people of all treaty nations requires that the parties take the steps necessary to eradicate the negative stereotypes and the effects flowing from them. First and foremost is the need to restore among First Nations peoples a positive sense of origin and belonging.

Mythologies have been created depicting First Nations as the original immigrants to the Americas. In part, these mythologies were created to justify the taking of First Nations' lands by Europeans. They also are intended to diminish and weaken the First Nations' sense of origin and belonging to "the Peoples' Island."

Elder Gordon Oakes was emphatic in his desire to see the negative impact of these colonial mythologies neutralized and indeed reversed. The Elders could not see how healing within First Nations could occur without a positive sense of identity and awareness of the healing gifts given to First Nations by the Creator.

The Elders also believe that Canada must take those measures necessary to reverse the negative stereotypes that European colonial policies and institutions have created of First Nations peoples. It is their view that "respect" is an essential pillar upon which good relations (*miyo-wîcêhtowin*) can be brought about. Without a positive and respectful view of First Nations peoples, good relations (*miyo-wîcêhtowin*) between First Nations peoples and others living in Canada cannot be achieved.

The Elders express a strong need for a comprehensive, long-term educational process both within First Nations and non-Aboriginal communities. Part of that process requires the development of educational and information programs designed to reflect and convey the full history of First Nations. Those programs must include accurate information describing in full the significance of the contributions made by First Nations to the development and evolution of Canada as a nation-state. Not the least of the First Nations contributions is the relationship with the Crown created in the treaties, which played an integral part of the development and growth of Canada.

The Elders point out that the complete history of North America and particularly of the First Nations still needs to be developed, including within that history the sense of origin that derives from the Creation stories of First Nations peoples. Establishing and recognizing the legitimacy of the First Nations perspective would begin to unravel the destructive effects of colonial mythology about First Nations. For First Nations, an initial step suggested for redressing the lost sense of origin and belonging entrenched by colonial mythology is to begin a process of highlighting the First Nations peoples own beliefs, including their sense of origin. All First Nations possess Creation histories that speak of their sense of origin and belonging to North America.

Elder Gordon Oakes of Nekaneet related the Creation story, according to his grandmother:

> She spoke of a previous human civilization before this one. The people of that ancient civilization were given far greater power by the Creator than this current civilization. For example, people could then fly. Those ancient people led themselves into a life of disrespect and they began to abuse their way of life.
>
> At that time, there existed four good

grandfather spirits who were responsible for that civilization. Due to the chaos of that ancient civilization, our Creator decided to discontinue them by causing a great flood.

After the flood, Grandfather Spirit (*Wîsahkêcâhk*) took some mud and from it he molded some men. He then addressed Our Father and said he molded the men but the men had no life in them. Then our Creator reminded *Wîsahkêcâhk* that He had provided him with a sacred life-giving whistle and instructed him to blow on it. When *Wîsahkêcâhk* blew on the sacred whistle, the women were created by our Creator and were spiritually put on earth to join the men.

The people began to propagate and at some point in time they formed a circle to meet. With the powers bestowed on them they began to take responsibilities and duties upon themselves with the other beings. This was the time when a young man offered himself to be a communicator to the Great Spirit and would become the sweetgrass and the moose offered himself to be the interpreter of peoples' prayers, but his offer was not accepted but the same offer by the rock was accepted.

The succeeding new civilization sought after those four loving grandfather spirits to help them as they were bestowed with less power than the other previous civilization. Those four grandfather spirits came from the four directions to love this new civilization and answered their prayers to teach them a way of life to survive. The people then could still fly, and they tried to fly upwards in hopes of meeting the Creator directly again for more direction, and the Creator instead took away their ability to fly and gave them various languages after which they then, according

Sweetgrass (Abraham Wikaskokiseyin), head chief of the Cree, 1877. Glenbow Archives

to their linguistic groups moved to settle throughout the Peoples' Island. The four grandfather spirits then bestowed these people, through the power of the Creator, with many sacred ceremonies and prayer lodges through which they could pray to the Creator and through which they could preserve their oral history and teachings. One of the most sacred gifts they bestowed is the Sundance and to this day four grandfather spirits are acknowledged and revered in the sacred pipe and other ceremonies.[39]

Simon Kytwayhat, a Cree Elder from Treaty 6, explained:

> The Indians had relationships with others such as our big brother (*Wîsahkêcâhk*). He was related to everyone and everything and every being was related to him and spoke of him. In fact, he was the one, they say, who created this island during a time of a big flood. I guess he used the help of animals. I think it was the beaver who first dove the flood waters, then the muskrat followed. The muskrat drowned, but he had a lump of mud on his paw. *Wîsahkêcâhk* blew on the mud. This is a story my parents (and my grandparents) used to tell me.[40]

All First Nations possess rich sources of oral history and information pertaining to their peoples and the lands occupied by their nations. The Elders, as custodians of that knowledge strongly indicated their readiness to share the knowledge they have. They stand prepared to help provide guidance, direction, and co-operation with any educational process that is designed to help re-instill the positive self-image so methodically taken away from First Nations peoples. They are prepared as well to assist in any public education program aimed at bringing about good relations (*miyo-wîcêhtowin*) between their peoples and other Canadians for they recognize that ignorance and Eurocentric arrogance breeds disrespect and without respect there can be no reconciliation.

© *Tourism Saskatchewan*

Kihci-asotamâtowin

Sacred Promises to One Another, The Treaty Sovereigns' Sacred Undertakings

The Elders have been unequivocal in their statement that the treaties cannot be changed or altered. Given the intensity with which the statement has been made regarding the unchangeable nature of the treaties, we spent a considerable amount of time in focus sessions examining the statement so that we could get a clearer sense about what is meant by the Elders' statements.[41]

In the focus sessions with the Elders, it became very clear that their view and understanding of the treaties differed significantly and substantively from the written text of the treaties. Indeed, their focus was on the "nature and character of the treaty relationship" as opposed to the contents of the written treaty texts created by the Crown.

The Elders continued to be adamant and insistent upon their view that the treaties cannot be changed or altered.

Elder Peter Waskahat of the Frog Lake First Nation stated:

> The [treaties] can only be broken through the will of the Creator.[42]

Elder Eli Adam of the Fond du Lac Denesuline Nation stated:

> What I want to maintain is what we promised and what was promised to us as

Elders speaking at the Treaty Elders Forum held in Wollaston Lake, November 3, 1997

Big Bear (c. 1825-1888; centre wearing an ostrich-plume hat) with some of his people and traders at Fort Pitt, 1884, after his return from Montana where he and many of his people lived from 1881 to 1883. Unwilling to enter treaty without his people present, Big Bear was put on trial in 1885 for treason and was imprisoned in Stony Mountain Penitentiary, Manitoba. In ill health, he was released from prison on January 27,1887. The Crown considered him and others to be rebels and refused to pay their annuities for a period of time after 1885. They were not allowed to leave the reserves without permits. Saskatchewan Archives Board

Chief Carry the Kettle, Treaty 4, 1910. Provincial Archives of Manitoba

Elder George Ryder, Carry the Kettle First Nation, Treaty 4

Elder Eli Adam, Fond du Lac Denesuline Nation, Treaty 8

Elder Danny Musqua, Keeseekoose First Nation, Treaty 4

long as the land lasts, so we are not going to let it go, we are going to hold onto it.[43]

Assiniboine Elder George Rider of the Carry the Kettle First Nation told us:

> The pipe is holy and it's a way of life for Indian people.... The treaty was made with a pipe and that is sacred, that is never to be broken ... never to be put away.[44]

Elder Norman Sunchild of the Thunderchild First Nation said:

> The Treaty Commissioner [Alexander Morris] said these promises were forever ... the Elders would say the treaties are very spiritually sacred including what was enshrined in [Divine] law by force of the treaty-making process.... Till the sun passes by, and this Saskatchewan River continues to flow, and the grass grows, those were the sacred promises. Those were the sacred words that they were using.... We are not to change anything.[45]

Elder Danny Musqua of the Keeseekoose First Nation stated:

> To be faithful to who you are is to be faithful to your Nation. If you are faithful to who you are, and your culture, and your language ... you follow the red road [and you are faithful to your Nation] because that is what the Creator made you to be. To be Cree. To be *Anishnâbê*.[46]

We are grateful to the Elders for the patience that they showed us during these focus sessions, particularly when the answers to the questions we posed may have seemed so self-evident to them. We found the focus sessions particularly helpful, and it is by and large from these sessions that we tried to frame the essential contours of

the Elders' statements. It is, however, important that a number of things be kept in mind:

First, the views expressed by the Elders are based on deeply held spiritual beliefs and philosophies. Given their historical experience with regard to the manner in which those beliefs were regarded by the Canadian state, the Elders are understandably cautious with respect to the amount, kind, and nature of information that they are prepared to share.

Second, the way knowledge is pursued and secured in the oral traditions of the First Nations is fundamentally different from such a pursuit in the larger society. The conceptual level at which these concepts were discussed requires a background understanding based on years of detailed, rigorous, disciplined training of the mind and body.

Conceptual and theoretical comprehension and discussion associated with any professional discipline, be it law or the medical profession, requires years of preparatory training accompanied by a rigorous discipline of studies. Without such preparation, it is difficult for anyone to understand or to comprehend many of the basic theories associated with those professions. Likewise, without proper preparation and study, it is difficult for anyone to understand the conceptual levels at which many of the Elders who participated in the process operate. Given the professional level at which these Elders function, they have been reluctant to discuss comprehensively many of the elements that require examination. This will continue to be so until they can be satisfied that a process has

Kahneepataytayo, Big Bear's head dancer. Saskatchewan Archives Board

been created that will facilitate the creation of a proper forum to allow for the proper exchange and transmission of such information to occur.

The presence of First Nations peoples in North America is seen by the Elders as evidence of the Creator's perfect love for the First Nations peoples. This perfect love gave birth to a continuing relationship between the Creator and the First Nations, which over time manifested itself in the transmission of whole and complete laws and institutions from Him to them. The presence of the perpetual life-giving and life-sustaining forces found in all aspects of Creation served both as evidence of this perfect love and a basis for the respect accorded to all the life forces of His Creation. The Elders tell us that the relationship between the First Nations and the Creator enabled them to meet all the physical and spiritual needs of First Nations as peoples and as individuals. The union created between the Creator and the First Nations was, in and of itself, complete and whole.

Elder Dolly Neapetung commented:

> The Creator gave us a way of life and a language by which we could speak to one another and speak to Him and to give meaning to everything that was around us ... to help us to understand the world and other people, our relatives.[47]

Elder Jacob Bill added:

> It is ... the Creator, who created everything, who put us here on this land.[48]

Elder Danny Musqua stated:

> Everything came from our Creator, all things, and all the laws ... we learned our

relationship in four orders [the Creator, the spiritual universe, the natural universe, and man as a universe].

> The Creator sets out the laws that govern our relationship[s] ... sets out all the ways by which to understand who is God and what He is, and how He created the universe and how we come from our Creator through a circle of life, and how we return there again.[49]

Elder Jimmy Myo said:

> When the Creator first put Indians on this land, He gave him everything that he needed, land to live on, He gave them trees, animals and from there to make his own clothing and to make their shelters and to eat. And He also put there good medicines that would heal all kinds of illnesses and those medicines were true and they were all good medicines.
>
> The Creator has given the Indians a lot of powerful things. And everything that He has given to the Indian is all meshed into a way of life.[50]

Elder Kay Thompson said:

> We are all part of the Creator. This relationship is sacred (*Ade Wakan Tunga*) and is respected through the pipe.[51]

Denesuline Acting Chief Victor Echodh said:

> We the Dene here, we were put here by the Creator on this earth to live with a certain purpose, with a certain way; we know that. We see that in our ways, our land, wildlife that provides for us.[52]

Both the arrival of the White man to First Nations' territories prior to the signing of the treaties and the knowledge derived from First Nations belief systems enabled the First Nations to anticipate and prepare for the time when formal relations would have to be created between them and the arriving non-Aboriginals.

Elder Peter Waskahat stated:

> Elders from many different tribes say they knew about the coming of the White man long before he arrived. They say that Elders and holy men among them prophesied that men would come with different ways, that these men would want to live among them. Long before the arrival of the White man, the First Nations discussed how they would live with the White man. There were extensive discussions to determine how the First Nations could peacefully co-exist with the newcomers. The Elders say that they knew the White man was coming across the sea from places where there was much bloodshed. On the island of the new world created by *Wîsahkêcâhk*, that way of life could not prevail. The island of North America was created so that peace could prevail. When the newcomers arrived, peace treaties would need to be negotiated.
>
> It was decided long before the White man arrived that the First Nations would treat the newcomers as relatives, as brothers and sisters. The First Nations had decided that they would live in peace and that they would share the land with these newcomers. The sacred earth could never be sold or given away, according to the principles of the First Nations, but it could be shared. The First Nations decided that the earth could be shared with the newcomers and that it could be shared to the depth of a plough blade. The earth could be shared so that everyone could peacefully co-exist.[53]

When the time arrived for treaty, the First Nations saw it as necessary that they clearly and unequivocally indicate that their relationship with the Creator would not be altered by these arrangements. They saw the treaty as a way of securing the Crown's guarantee that the Crown would respect the integrity of the First Nations relationship with the Creator. They understood that the treaty parties would continue to be bound by the Creator's laws underlying the relationship with First Nations peoples.

Elder Jimmy Myo said:

> They told us that ... you would not be deterred from living your way of life. Our land, wildlife, the way we live [wouldn't] be altered, and we [wouldn't] be bothered over it.[54]

* * *

(*i*). The first principle affirmed by the treaties was the joint acknowledgement by the treaty-makers of the supremacy of the Creator and their joint fidelity to that divine sovereignty. This was in part the meaning of the ceremonies conducted by the First Nations during the treaty ceremonies where they used the pipe and the sweetgrass.

In the pipe ceremony, treaty parties signified their oneness in the undertaking that nations represented in the treaty would place their new relationship created by treaty in the hands of the Creator.

The sweetgrass used in the ceremony represented an undertaking between the parties that their relationship would be governed and conducted according to the principles symbolized by the sweetgrass and the pipe. The symbols used by First Nations contain complex and

Chief Poundmaker and Governor David Laird meet at Battleford, 1880. RCMP Museum, Regina, Saskatchewan

Assiniboine Indian Council near Fort Walsh. Glenbow Archives

Elder Simon Kytwayhat,
Makwa Sahgaiehcan
First Nation, Treaty 6

Elder Bart McDonald,
Fond du Lac
Denesuline Nation,
Treaty 8

comprehensive meanings. The Elders referred to some of the values and principles underlying them.

These included, among others, the following First Nations principles:

manâtisiwin	respect
yôspâtisiwin	gentleness
kisêwâtisiwin	kindness
kwayaskâtisiwin	honesty and fairness
kanâtisiwin	cleanliness

These are but a few of the values and principles that were to guide the treaty relationship as it evolved between the treaty parties – an undertaking at the fundamental level that the relations between the parties would be non-coercive, non-adversarial, and non-antagonistic.

Elder Danny Musqua said:

> We made a covenant with Her Majesty's government, and a covenant is not just a relationship between people, it's a relationship between three parties, you [the Crown] and me [First Nations] and the Creator.[55]

Elder Peter Waskahat said:

> In the initial discussions taking place, the first time, between the Indian and the non-Indian, the Holy Spirit language was used. When the Indian spoke to the non-Indian [they exchanged] ... vows. [The non-Indian said] your way of worship, I will respect it ... I agree to that ... [it was] a mutual agreement....
>
> In their [ways of] worship, they [the parties of treaty] are talking about the Creator, understanding, communication, worshipping the Creator [each in his own] way.[56]

(ii). The second irrevocable undertaking of the treaty relationship was the commitment between the parties to maintain a relationship of peace. The Elders described the nature of these sacred undertakings to the Creator in the following ways:

Cree Elder Simon Kytwayhat said:

> When our cousins (*kiciwâminawak*) the White man, first came to peacefully live on these lands (*wîtaskêmâcik*) with the Indigenous people, the [Elders] used the pipe, sweetgrass and the pipe stem.... And when they took the traditional adoption with the White man, they used the pipe and they shared the pipe with them from where they adopted a peaceful existence (*wîtaskêwin*).[57]

The undertakings were anchored in these sacred undertakings (pipe, sweetgrass, pipe stem) made to the Creator.

Dene Elder Bart McDonald (Treaty 8) said:

> Let's live together in peace and harmony. And let's remember the Creator, who created all these things, all the resources, why He created everything for us.[58]

Elder Jacob Bill said:

> We say it's our Father (*wiyôhtâwîmâw*); the White man says "our Father" in his language, so from there we should understand that he becomes our brother and we have to live harmoniously with him. There should not be any conflict, we must uphold the word "*wîtaskêwin,*" which means to live in peace and harmony with one another.[59]

Peace, according to First Nations definitions, is more than just an undertaking that there would be no war between the parties. The First Nations terms speak to the positive undertaking of the parties to nurture and root their treaty relationship in the principles of good, healthy, happy, respectful relationships (*miyo-wîcêhtowin*) as symbolized by the laws governing relationships between cousins.

Elder Norman Sunchild described the treaty as:

> *Okimâw miyo-wîcihitowiyêcikêwin, wîtaskê-osihcikêwin* – an agreement between the sovereign leaders to establish good relations and to live together in peace.[60]

(*iii*). The third irrevocable undertaking of the treaty was the mutual agreement to initiate and to create a perpetual familial relationship based on familial concepts defined by the First Nations principles of *wâhkôhtowin* (good relationships). These relationships were to be conducted and regulated by the principles and laws governing familial relationships (*wîtisânîhitowin*). The Elders described the nature of this relationship in the following ways:

Elder Simon Kytwayhat said:

> When our cousins, the White man, first came to peacefully live on these lands (*ê-wîtaskêmâcik*) with the Indigenous people, as far as I can remember, Elders have referred to them as "*kiciwâminawak*" (our first cousins). I have heard [from my Elders] that the Queen came to offer a traditional adoption of us as our mother. "You will be my children," she had said.[61]

© *Tourism Saskatchewan*

Treaty 8 Medal; courtesy of the Ethnology Program, Provincial Museum of Alberta, Edmonton, Alberta

Elder Peter Waskahat said:

> And when this Treaty Commissioner [Morris] came here [in 1876], my Elder used to tell me ... he came here to offer himself to be our first cousin, like in Cree – *niciwâm*.[62]

Elder Danny Musqua said:

> The Queen has adopted [First Nations] as children ... a joint relationship will come out of that. And so we have a joint relationship with the Crown because the Queen is now our mother.[63]

Elder Jimmy Myo said:

> They said, we came here as your relatives. They said, the Queen sent us here, the Queen wants to adopt you Indians ... as her own children.[64]

Elder Alma Kytwayhat said:

> It was the [Queen] who offered to be our mother and us to be her children and to love us in the way we want to live[65]

For the Elders, the use of these familial terms to describe the nature of the treaty relationship meant, among other things, that the relationship between the First Nations and the Crown and their respective peoples would follow the rules and laws governing what is called in the Cree language "*wâhkôhtowin*" (good relationships). All of the different treaty nations possess similar doctrines of laws governing conduct within relationships. These are rules and laws that prescribe and proscribe conduct covering a wide range of relationships. They are comprehensive in that they contain detailed codes of behaviour, setting out what is prohibited, what is encouraged, the values that are to be respected and followed in each set of relations.

As an example, the Cree doctrine of *wâhkôhtowin* sets out an unwritten code of conduct, which, among other things, sets out the conduct and behaviour that must be maintained between:

- *a mother and child:* the principle of mutual respect which entailed the reciprocal duties of nurturing, caring, loyalty, and fidelity;
- *family members – brothers and sisters:* relationships regulated by the laws of kinship, which recognized the close yet separate and independent existence of each and which provided for the principle of non-interference;
- *cousins and other relatives:* setting out behaviour that was permitted and not permitted – social codes of behaviour setting out the relationships that were to be maintained between uncles and nephews, aunts and nieces, and cousins – the relationship codes encouraged respectful though less stringent codes of behaviour that allowed the persons to maintain happy and non-coercive relations;
- *unrelated persons:* codes that required *manâtisiwin* (being respectful) and *manâcihitowin* (treating each other with care and respect).

(*iv*). The fourth irrevocable undertaking between and among the parties was the guarantee of each other's survival and stability anchored on the principle of mutual sharing:

Elder Jacob Bill said:

> It was the will of the Creator that the White man would come here and live with us, among us to share our lives together

Cree camp south of Vermillion, 1871. National Archives of Canada

Senator Allan Bird,
Montreal Lake
Cree Nation, Treaty 6

The late Elder Martin Mark Josie,
Hatchet Lake Denesuline Nation,
Treaty 10

with him, and also both of us collectively, to benefit from the bounty of Mother Earth for all time to come and for himself so that there is enough for him to make a living from the bounty, but equally with the Indians. That is the value and the true nature and spirit and intent of the treaty on both sides, and it's on both for both to benefit.[66]

(*v*). The fifth irrevocable undertaking was that the sharing arrangement would guarantee to the First Nations and their citizens a continuing right of livelihood.

Elder Martin Josie said:

And other things as well, wildlife, land, we don't want you to talk about us over that, we want to ensure that our abilities to carry on with our way of life over our lands will always be there, and always be protected for the future generations. But you did not buy that from us, you have to remember that. And [we] were assured of that, our people were assured that was not to be, that our way of life would always continue, as well our ability to hunt, harvest the resources off of the land, would be protected for all further generations. That is what I remember the Elders speaking about when I was young.[67]

Elder Norman Sunchild said:

It was understood that the Queen had given Alexander Morris instructions to say ... go tell them that I am not asking for anything, just his land for the purpose of Her Majesty's subjects to make a livelihood upon these lands. And everything else where he [the Indian people] lives, those things continue to belong to him and nobody can control that for him.[68]

Elder Peter Waskahat said:

The Commissioner had said, it is not all your land I am interested in. Only the places where my people will be coming on those lands down to the depth of a plough, that is what I am asking for. The minerals ... you will continue to be owners of that.
I did not come here to ask for your wildlife. You know since the beginning of time when the earth was first created and when our Creator put you here that you had this for your sustenance; you still continue to own them. No one with two legs will ever come and punish you over the use of them, he had said. Anything that flies, from where you get your sustenance in life, I didn't come to ask for that....
All the creatures under the water, that too, I didn't come to ask you for it. That will continue to be yours from where you can gain life.
The timber, I only want for my personal use or for use on my farmland.
Your way of life and how you survive from this and how you look after yourself you will always continue to have, that is not what I am asking of you.[69]

Elder Gordon Oakes said:

Our land is plentiful.... [At treaty they said] I will bring farmers from another land. From there, I will get money to help you. There's lots of things that she promised: education, health, housing, school, blankets, farm implements, what the Indian can use to make a living. These are the things that were promised.[70]

Senator Allan Bird said:

At the time, the government said that we would live together, that I am not here to take away what you have now.... I am here to borrow the land ... to the depth of a plough ... that is how much I want.[71]

The principles of mutual sharing are rooted in the belief systems of the First Nations. Mutual sharing meant first and foremost that the parties would share with one another some elements of the special gifts accorded to them by the Creator.

For the First Nations, such a sharing required not only human consent – it required legitimization and sanction by and through the spiritual traditions of the First Nations. This was in much evidence at the treaty-making ceremonies. The Elders point to the spiritual symbols, which were essential elements in the treaty-making process.

Elder Jimmy Myo said:

> We hear from old people how powerful our spiritual life is, and that's what is going to help us....We have to pray like an Indian, believe in our way of life.... When that is gone, that is a sign that our treaties are gone because our treaties are part of our cultural and spiritual traditions and our Indian laws.[72]

Elder Jacob Bill said:

> That is where the traditional Indian is very afraid of the ending of a treaty because it wasn't the will of human beings that made this treaty as to why we are sharing this land with the White man.[73]

Elders in the northern part of the province refer to the medallions that were presented at treaty depicting two figures shaking hands in friendship against the backdrop of the symbols of the sun, the grass, and the river.

Elder Celeste Randhill said:

> The medallion that I have here is one that my dad gave me to hold onto, to protect, and it's one similar to the one that he has. It is similar to the big one that he used to have and what he used to say is, whenever you talk about our rights and our ways, our treaties, and so on, it's important for me to show it to you here because our word (the promises that we have made) has not been broken yet and by taking that out and as well as the symbolic strength of the medallion such as that is that it cannot be broken easily and same with our word as well too. It is important that we carry on with our word and to remind people that we have not ... broken our word yet, we still go by our word today. For me anyway, what I have done with you today is share information on what my dad told me and what he had wished for his people in terms from some sort of homeland for his people as well as protection of rights for the Denesuline in the far North....
>
> Like I said already, our ways are very important to us, and, in the North, we still strongly believe in our ways. We still carry on our practices of traditional harvesting as well as hunting and different harvesting. Methods we have always utilized, we still do that, we teach them to our young people. We make every effort to make our word heard as Elders, and I'm pretty sure just by doing that we pretty well fulfilled our side in terms of transferring information from the old generation to the younger generation about the importance of things such as treaties and harvesting of the wildlife products as well as using our land as we promised we would do.

Elder Celeste Randhill, Fond du Lac Denesuline Nation, Treaty 8

Senator Hilliard Ermine, Sturgeon Lake First Nation, Treaty 6

Chief Thunderchild (c.1916) was originally part of a very large following that moved with Big Bear. In 1876, he and several others including Lucky Man and Little Pine stood as leaders of their own groups and entered Treaty at Fort Walsh. He went north and settled in the Battleford Agency area. He is wearing his Treaty medal and also the smaller Queen Victoria medal, given to chiefs who remained peaceful during the 1885 Resistance.
Saskatchewan Archives Board

Before my dad died, he strongly believed in the establishment of a traditional area for the Denesuline and the Chipewyan Nation and he had it all drawn out on a big map ... [with] the treaty medallion and he had stored with some people up in Fort Smith, Northwest Territories.[74]

Senator Allan Bird said:

They [the Elders] were given great wisdom, they did not go to school, but they were given wisdom from the Spirit, the Great Spirit ... that is why they used the water, the grass, and the sun. And what was said was, until those things do not exist, that our treaties should exist for as long as those things exist.[75]

* * *

The fundamental principles identified by the Elders constitute aspects of the treaty relationship that, in their view, are not subject to change or alteration between the parties.

Their understanding of these principles are interwoven with and derive their existence from the spiritual and ceremonial fabric of First Nations societies. They provide the contextual framework for the Indian understanding of the collective and individual relationships created by treaty.

These First Nations conceptual foundations speak to the ideals, norms, values, and principles that informed and guided the conduct of the treaty nations at the time the treaties were negotiated. They represent a First Nations conceptual framework for understanding First Nations notions of inter-nation relationships. They are at the same time the source of First Nations theoretical perspectives with regard to notions of civic duties and responsibilities. Properly approached and considered, they provide a basis for understanding the First Nations notion of freedom, individual rights, and obligations.

The Elders have indicated that they are prepared to continue providing information on these matters. They have identified initial principles, and it is in subsequent settings where the details must be further examined.

We tried, in a preliminary manner, to capture the essence of the message delivered by the Elders regarding the aspects of treaty which they felt were not to be changed in perpetuity as reflected in the phrase "as long as the sun shines, the rivers flow, the grass grows or as long as the sun shines, the rivers flow, and the rock does not move."

The importance of these messages was emphasized and re-emphasized throughout the Treaty Elders Forums:

Senator Hilliard Ermine said:

And the old people that made the treaties, they're the ones that told us not to fool around with these treaties, they're very important.[76]

Elder Jacob Bill said:

When one makes a sacred promise to the Creator ... such an undertaking is a grave matter, and it is to be feared in the event of a breach.[77]

Wîtaskêwin
Living Together on the Land

"*Wîtaskêwin*" is a Cree word meaning "living together on the land." It is a word that has multiple applications and multidimensional meanings. It can include or refer to individuals or nations who are strangers to one another, agreeing to either live on or share for some specific purpose a land area with each other, or it can be applied to land-sharing arrangements between individual members of the nation.

However, in the context of treaty-making, "*wîtaskêwin*" refers to nations who are strangers to one another entering into agreements for the purposes of sharing land or territory with each other.

Before the treaties with the Crown, First Nations entered into formal agreements or treaties with one another for the purposes of establishing peaceful relations and territorial sharing arrangements. Within each of their own conceptual contexts, they had clear notions of their existence as political communities or nations.

Elder Danny Musqua said:

> All of the agreements they have had between one another as peoples and as nations were always based on [land] use – on how they were going to use that land.
>
> And ... when I say that the use of that land, we had agreements between one another, hunting territories that we shared, trapping lands that we shared, gathering lands that we shared, medicinal lands that we shared [sacred lands], peace territorial lands that we designated for the shelter and safety of all people.
>
> And [the boundaries of] those lands were always laid out before these peoples.... That's how they set out things between one another. They understood use; they understood the means by which land was used.[78]

It was understood that the White man would bring his own animals and that the animals on the land prior to the treaties were to continue to be there for the First Nations.

Each of the First Nations had, and continues to have, clearly defined notions of who they are as a people. This is reflected both in their linguistic definitions of themselves and in the spiritual traditions that provide a theoretical context or framework for them.

In each of their languages, the Elders described the collectivity of their citizenry in the following terms: Elder Jacob Bill describes the Cree as "*Nêhiyawak*," a Cree term meaning "people of the four directions."[79] Elder Peter Waskahat uses another term: "*Iyiniwak*," a Cree term meaning "people made healthy by the land."[80] Elder Kay Thompson describes the Assiniboine as: "*Anina Ombi*," an Assiniboine term describing themselves as silent people,

Chipewyan Indians, 1899. Glenbow Archives

people who go around silently. "*Wadopana*," is another Assiniboine term referring to canoe people. "*Nakoda*" is an Assiniboine term designating all other Indian peoples.[81] Elder John B. Bigeye stated that his people call themselves "*Denesuline*," the people, or the real people.[82] Elder Danny Musqua stated that the Saulteaux call themselves "*Anishnâbê*," which means "coming down to be men/man; the First People that came down from the Creator."[83]

The Elders described some of the spiritual traditions through which First Nations nationhood, sovereignty, and relationship with the Creator has been (and continues to be) affirmed, reaffirmed, and renewed. For example, some of the Elders point to those aspects of the Sundance (an annual ceremony conducted among the prairie tribes) that symbolize the renewal and affirmation of First Nations sovereignty continuing First Nations fidelity to the Creator.

The Sundance is a sacred First Nations ceremony. The teachings associated with it are many and complex, only some of which can be shared. For the purposes of the present treaty process, the Elders have decided that they would share some of the teachings to try and assist others to better understand the First Nations perspective of treaty. The Elders referred to two aspects of the Sundance, which in their view might assist in understanding First Nations perspectives. These relate to the physical layout of the Sundance encampment and some of the fundamental laws that are affirmed by it.

Elders Jimmy Myo, Jacob Bill, and Gordon Oakes tell us that the Sundance encampment symbolizes the coming together of the nation or nations to reaffirm and renew their fidelity to the relationship held with the Creator.[84] It is both a collective and individual act of renewal and reaffirmation.

The Sundance lodge, which is located at the centre of the encampment, represents the unity between the Creator, his Creation, and the First Nations. The many complex and interrelated ceremonies conducted within it represent the core or essential acts of renewal required of First Nations and their people.

Qu'Appelle Valley

© *Ted Whitecalf*

Elders Jimmy Myo, Jacob Bill, and Gordon Oakes tell us that the circular encampment of tents or teepees around the Sundance lodge represents the forming of a circle and the coming together of peoples.[85]

The setting up of the encampment and the ceremonies that accompany it represent an individual and collective undertaking, renewing and refurbishing the people's relationship with one another and with the Creator and His Creation. The acts of renewal represent a sacred undertaking by the individuals and the nations to renew and strengthen their relationships with one another under the laws of *wâhkôhtowin* (relationship).

In this sense, through the Sundance ceremonies, First Nations continually reaffirm and renew the sovereignty aspect of the relationships given to them by their Creator. They symbolize and represent the existence of a living, sovereign First Nations circle.

The linguistic definitions and ceremonial contexts both provide a framework within which First Nations definitions of the terms "peoples," "distinct political communities," or "sovereign peoples" are to be understood. The meanings originate in the spiritual traditions of each of the First Nations. They form foundational components for "*wîtaskêwin*" – a term that refers, in this context, to peoples establishing relationships that are to be governed by the laws of *wâhkôhtowin* and which are reflected in the kinds of land-sharing arrangements created between the parties.

Elder Gordon Oakes said:

> And the relationships between *wîcihitowin* and *wîtaskêwin*, they are all the same. They all have the same connotation with respect to the relations of the land.[86]

The Elders were very clear in their presentations that they see their sovereign political communities as originating from the Creator and continuing in the particular spiritual relationships that each of the nations continues to maintain with the Creator and His Creation through their various spiritual traditions and their connectedness to the land.

Senator Hilliard Ermine said:

> You see, [we] Indian people, we have law; it's not man-made law; that law we have was given to us by God.[87]

Elder Gordon Oakes said:

> When the White man came upon North America, they realized that this land belonged to the Indians. It was given ... Indians were put here and given this North America island, and it was theirs.[88]

The treaties, through the spiritual ceremonies conducted during the negotiations, expanded the First Nations sovereign circle, bringing in and embracing the British Crown within their sovereign circle. The treaties, in this view, were arrangements between nations intended to recognize, respect, and acknowledge in perpetuity the sovereign character of each of the treaty parties, within the context of rights conferred by the Creator to the Indian nations. The rituals followed in the ceremonies

Elder John B. Bigeye, Black Lake Denesuline Nation, Treaty 8

Elder George Cannepotato, Onion Lake First Nation, Treaty 6

Indian Agent for Treaty 5 paying treaty money, Little Grand Rapids, 1925. Provincial Archives of Manitoba

conducted during the treaty negotiations and sacred undertakings made under the umbrella of those ceremonies created enduring sovereign relationships in a manner that precluded change by any of the parties to the fundamental aspects of the treaty arrangements.

Elder Peter Waskahat said:

> The indigenous person was given a lot by the Creator ... [treaty] agreement that will last and cannot be broken by a two-legged person. It can only be broken through the will of the Creator.[89]

Elder Celeste Randhill said:

> Today is another example, based on the signing of the treaty, everybody is asking for one purpose, and that's towards anything that's got to do with helping us Dene people. We have this one voice here, and everybody's got the same story. What the Queen (or was it the King?) agreed on the treaty, we are not going to abolish that; we will respect that. We will always respect the treaties and all the things that are involved in that. It doesn't matter even though they try and take different rights from us, we'll still hang onto our rights, and we'll preserve it as much as we can.[90]

The treaties are instruments that expanded the sovereign First Nations circle to accommodate and include the sovereign Crown. These arrangements are, in the view of the Elders, nation-to-nation agreements.

Elder George Cannepotato said:

> The Treaty Commissioner had come over to shake their hands, and the Commissioner offered to be related to them, and he wanted the rest of the White people to have a

relationship with them ... in our way we made those commitments through and in the name of and in the force of the pipe stem. And it was the pipe stem that the chiefs had Alexander Morris hold who came as the representative. That is our solemn way of doing promises.[91]

The statement "treaties cannot be changed" refers to the sacred undertakings made by the parties at treaty. These undertakings included, in part, territorial and power-sharing arrangements between the sovereign authorities. Such arrangements require a foundation of stability, continuity, and certainty. The irrevocable nature of the arrangement provided such a guarantee to each of the treaty parties.

* * *

Having described the Elders' concerns and thoughts on the perpetual character of the treaties, we now turn to consider those aspects or elements of treaty that, in their view, required flexibility and adaptability in accordance with changing times. Some of the Elders referred to a promise that these elements or matters would be dealt with in the future by the parties.

Elder Gordon Oakes said:

> As I was saying about the depth of the plough, the Treaty Commissioner [Alexander Morris] also advised that some day he will be mining valuable minerals and at the time I will come back and negotiate with you again on it. You have not followed your promise when you said that you would return to conclude other unfinished treaty business.[92]

Pimâcihowin
Making a Living

During the course of the treaty meetings, the Elders focussed a substantial amount of their time on questions that they felt were fundamental to the survival and well-being of their children, grandchildren, and future generations of First Nations peoples. Central to their concern was the need for First Nations to re-establish or reassert their connection to traditional lands and territories, a connection that many saw as constituting a critically important component of the treaty relationship with the Crown.

This connection to the land, as described by the Elders, consists of at least the following elements: spiritual, physical, and economic. This connection is rooted in the Cree concept and doctrines related to *pimâtisiwin* (life). It is a concept that contains many theoretical subsets including among other things, a concept called "*pimâcihowin*" (the ability to make a living). Land (*askiy*) is an important source of life for it provides those things required for the physical, material, and economic survival of the people.

When treaty Elders use the word "*pimâcihowin*," they are describing a holistic concept that includes a spiritual as well as a physical dimension. It is an integral component of traditional First Nations doctrines, laws, principles, values, and teachings regarding the sources of life, the responsibilities associated with them, including those elements seen as necessary for enhancing the spiritual components of life and those associated with making a living.

The Dene, Cree, Saulteaux, and Assiniboine Treaty First Nations in Saskatchewan share a common philosophy and a common conceptual basis in what their Elders refer to as a way of life, making a living or livelihood. It is a philosophy that speaks to a particular, unique First Nations world vision of connectedness, which many Elders believed was protected and guaranteed by treaty.

When Elders describe the wealth of the land in terms of its capacity to provide a livelihood, they are referring not simply to its material capabilities but also to the spiritual powers that are inherent in it. This includes all the elements of Creation that the Creator gave to the First Peoples: Mother Earth, the sun, air, water, fire, trees, plant life, rocks, and all the animals.

Elder Dolly Neapetung stated:

> We were able to look after ourselves through the use of these gifts that God gave us, our ability to feed ourselves and look after our children. We were proud of ourselves because we took care of ourselves, we had the animals to hunt, we had the

Fur press at Fond du Lac, Saskatchewan, c. 1903-06. Glenbow Archives

The late Elder Bart Dzeylion, Hatchet Lake Denesuline Nation, Treaty 10

© *Tourism Saskatchewan*

food that God put on the land, the berries and the medicines that we carried out and that we go out and gather.[93]

Elder Danny Musqua said:

This old man gets up, and he says to the Commissioner [Alexander Morris] "what about the lands that I hold sacred?" He was talking about his hunting territories, the fishing territories, the gathering territories. "All those things that I use that I hold sacred for my survival and my peoples [survival]."

Commissioner Morris said: "We don't want [sacred lands, and territories used for survival] ... we will keep these lands for you; we will protect these lands for you so that only you can use them in time of difficulty and hardship at any time in the future.[94]

Elder John James Mercredi commented:

When we were promised as part of the treaty negotiations that you would carry on with your way of life, and no one would bother you for it, that is how we are going to stand today. We're not going to back down because we believe that the land is our life.[95]

Elder Bart McDonald said:

This land is our land. The Dene land. We are People of the Land. The land is who we are. The wildlife provides for us. Fish, water, trees, everything, the plants, all the animals, all the beings of the Earth all provide for us. We lived off that. That was part of our livelihood.[96]

Elder Bart Dzeylion:

What we do know is there's two important things: lands and resources and we knew that, we knew what the land meant to us, we knew what the wildlife meant to us ... other things and not relevant to our way of life, the land, the wildlife, those are the things that were relevant to our people of the day. When our people were assured that those ways of life would not be altered or changed or that we would not be deterred from exercising those ways of life, that way of life, then I know that from the information that I have, that our people agreed through that process. So to relations to the land, that's the type of information that I can add to the discussions. Our land, our way of life, would always be protected, would always be there, is what I have for information from my mother.[97]

The teaching of respect associated with the concept of *pimâcihowin* provided guidance for the ways in which individuals conducted themselves when exercising their duty to provide for their life needs from the gifts provided by the Creator. These teachings are central to the personal and skill training provided by First Nations to enable their peoples to achieve independence in terms of providing for their needs, those of their families and those of their communities.

The teachings related to self-sufficiency (*tipiyawêwisowin*) provided to the individual direction and guidance and set out the requirements for achieving a sense of self-worth, dignity, and independence – values that were and are essential to a community's or a nation's internal peace, harmony, and security. The teachings (*kakêskihkêmowina*) included unwritten but well-known codes of behaviour for the Cree people in relation to *pimâcihisowin* (making one's own living).

They contained codes of personal conduct designed to enable one to "make his or her own living." For example, the code, among other things, describes those characteristics that each person was encouraged to acquire:

iyinîsiwin:	the ability to develop a keen mind
nahihtamowin:	the ability to develop keen sense of hearing
nahâsiwin:	the ability to develop alert and discerning faculties
nisitohtamowin:	the ability to develop understanding
kakayiwâtisiwin:	the ability to develop an inner sense of industriousness or inner ability or desire to be hardworking
astoskêwimahcihowin:	the inner desire or need to work
waskawîwin:	inner energy to move or develop a sense of personal initiative
manâtisiwin:	the inner capacity of respect
kisêwâtisiwin:	the capacity to be kind

The connection to the land, to Mother Earth, was indispensable to the First Nations peoples if they were to achieve the ability to make a living and meet the responsibilities demanded of them by the spiritual values contained in the codes of their nations.

Elder Kay Thompson said:

> We knew what to take. We didn't kill for nothing ... we gave it all to each other; they were caring about one another.... We wanted to be allowed to look after ourselves according to treaty [to be self-sufficient].[98]

Elder August Lidguerre said:

> The land is very valuable to us. It is very valuable, all the wildlife, all the furs, animals, what animals are here. If our people were mismanaging the wildlife, the wildlife resources that the Creator put on the earth for us, if we mismanaged it, there wouldn't be anything left for us today.[99]

Elder Celeste Randhill said:

> My grandfathers and my great-grandfathers were travelling up in the Northwest Territories. I remember, they used to tell me all those stories. And we used to follow caribou and then where the musk-ox are that is a long ways. That's our livelihood ... that's how they used to bring their canoes here and then take over the dog team ... used to follow one another and go to a river called Thelon River. They travelled across the river, and then just take all the necessities, take the hides from the musk-ox and keep the bones and anything that can be used for tools and so forth. From then to this day, people didn't change their minds. If they went out hunting ... nobody told us this is how you hunt musk-ox ... and the government didn't tell us this is how you are going to hunt ... and they didn't have any rules or regulations imposed. They didn't say we will give you a permit to go hunting on musk-ox. Nobody gave us any information in terms of how to hunt musk-ox.[100]

Denesuline Elder Louie Benoanie from Hatchet Lake said:

> The people loved their land, they wanted to keep their land, they wanted to live on their land. The way we live, we don't want them to be bothered by it. The runway, the water, the fish, the water-

Elder Louie Benoanie, Hatchet Lake Denesuline Nation, Treaty 10

Elder August Lidguerre, Fond du Lac Denesuline Nation, Treaty 8

Elder Pat Robillard, Black Lake Denesuline Nation, Treaty 8

Beardy, Cree Chief, 1885. He was known as a vocal critic of government, especially when the supplies promised for agriculture were not forthcoming. Glenbow Archives

fowl, everything we don't want to be bothered by exercising our traditional way of life. If you can guarantee us that he will make the treaty as what the people want and that's what I understand of the treaties. The way I look at it, the way I understand it today.[101]

Elder Dolly Neapetung said:

My grandmother told me there would be things like this in the future. That we would be hurt by it, and it would destroy us and it would destroy our people and destroy our children. Even in the things that we eat and the way that we eat today. Even in that we are sick from those things. We have sicknesses because of the things that we now eat. Because we never ate that way before. We used to live off the land and live off the fruit of the land. We ate wild meat and ate the fruits and berries that were there and were healthy because of it. Today, we're sick because of that. It seems today that young people do not understand and so therefore do not listen, and it's hard for them to understand when they don't listen. Because there are so many things that cause them difficulty that take them away from listening to us and listening to the old people.[102]

Elder Pat Robillard said:

We are still hanging [on] to our promises with them, but they're the ones that turn their backs on us and forgot about us.[103]

Elder Pauline Mercredi said:

We used to go to the Northwest Territories over sixty portages. We were using canoe, travelling. Men used to haul grub, material, all the necessities. And us women too we used to haul the things along with our mothers. And once we arrived where the caribou is that is how we survived. As soon as we meet the caribou, wherever they are we respect them.... That was our main source of food, and our clothing, providing clothing. Yes, we are known as the "caribou eaters."[104]

The sacred and spiritual qualities of these concepts are acknowledged continually in almost every one of the First Nations ceremonies, which express gratitude for the bounty of Mother Earth and the generosity of the Creator.

The Elders say they are still spiritually wealthy through their ceremonial connection to the sacred powers of Mother Earth. It is in this context and with their First Nations knowledge of the wealth that lay in the world around them that the treaty guarantees of livelihood must be understood.

Pimâcihowin: the treaty guarantees the continuing right of First Nations livelihood, and the continuing right of First Nations to maintain a continuing relationship to the land, and its resources constitutes one of the irrevocable and unchanging elements of the treaty relationship negotiated by First Nations and the Crown. These guarantees now embedded in the Canadian constitution were critical elements of the treaty negotiations in the latter part of the 1800s and continue to be critical to First Nations survival and well-being in the present and in the future.

For the Elders, the livelihood arrangements in treaties were intended to enable First Nations to continue their relationship to the land and to enable them to adapt to and become part of new modes of livelihood, which would accompany the fruition of their treaty relationship.

Elder Danny Musqua said:

> We believed that the treaties and the Crown were going to do us good. That they were going to bring the heart [the goodness and wealth] of the Great White Mother, the great Queen Mother, we believed that.... In 1905, it hadn't yet materialized. And when treaty implementation materialized, it was very limited. Some of our people became very good at what they had hoped they would acquire through these settlements. They became cattlemen. Animal husbandry was one of the very basic skills that our people had.... They knew how to take care of their animals....
>
> First Nations were clear and told the Crown ... we don't want your language. We don't want your [burial] grounds. We don't want your governments....
>
> The answer from Morris was "What you have shall be. We will maintain what you have and then we will put promises and protection on top of what you have. And what is that on top? All of these things that we said and the protection of the Crown. The Queen's authority shall surround you. She will protect you from all of these people here [newcomers]. She will protect you from encroachment of taxpayers, and land speculators ... she will protect you from the certain encroachment on your personal lives and your culture ... and from the settlers that will come ... and you will be just as wealthy as they are."[105]

What is consistently clear from most of the Elders' presentations is that a return to these fundamental principles is necessary if the present and future health of First Nations and their peoples is to be realized. The livelihood arrangements of treaty must be the basis for bringing back on track the treaty relationship, which seemed to have become lost somewhere in the entrails of colonial history.

Indian women in a canoe. Saskatchewan Archives Board

Tâpwêwin
Speaking the Truth or Speaking with Precision and Accuracy

The Record of Treaties 4, 5, 6, 8, and 10

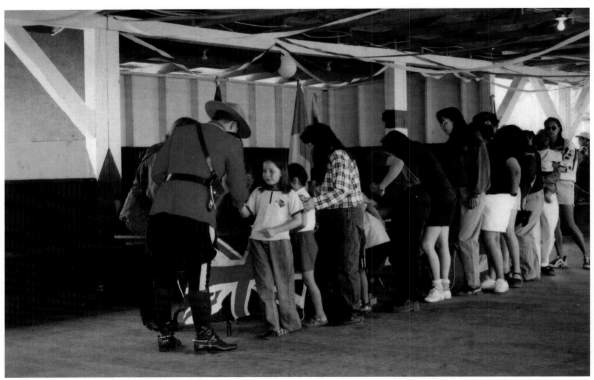

Clearwater River Treaty Days, 1998.   © *Office of the Treaty Commissioner*

"*Tâpwêwin*" is a Cree word meaning, "speaking the truth" or "speaking with precision and accuracy." Strict First Nations laws require that the duty or obligation to speak the truth (*tâpwêwin*) be meticulously followed when a subject matter has been considered and dealt with through the spiritual traditions and ceremonies of the nation.

The treaties are such subject matters. First Nations Elders, as indeed is the case with all representatives of the treaty signatories, are obligated to use "*tâpwêwin*" when they deal with the subject of the treaties. Consequently, they want to have the opportunity to discuss the subject matter with great care and with careful consideration.

A real problem exists with respect to the treaties – there is no formal existing agreement between the Crown and the First Nations as to the meaning and content of the treaties. It is a problem that needs to be addressed and resolved, if the spirit and intent of the treaty relationship is to be properly implemented.

At present, written documents purporting to be the official copies of the Indian treaties are published or recorded as follows:

1. written manuscripts of Treaties 4, 5, 6, 8, and 10 held in the National Archives of Canada;

2. copies of Treaties 4, 5, 6, 8, and 10 published by the Queen's printer.

Under the *Canada Evidence Act* (Section 20), those written documents are deemed to be the official copies of the treaties:

> Imperial proclamations, orders in council, treaties, orders, warrants, licences, certificates, rules, regulations or other Imperial official records, Acts or documents may be proved
>
> (c) by the production of a copy thereof purporting to be printed by the Queen's Printer.[106]

To date, Canada, particularly in litigation, takes the position that only "the articles of treaty" as contained in the Queen's Printer documents and as read literally can be used as the basis for determining whether or not there is an existing treaty right.

Such an approach would preclude the use of other sources for determining the content of the treaties like:

1. the Indian understanding of the treaties,
2. the Treaty Commissioners reports and dispatches,
3. eyewitness accounts of treaty negotiations, and
4. other related historical documents or correspondence.

Many legal firms and government officials rely exclusively on the so-called articles of treaty to identify and determine the kinds of rights, obligations, duties, and relationships contained in the treaties.

© *Tourism Saskatchewan*

Almost Spring at Meadow Lake   © *Darrell Seib*

Chief Cote, one of the prominent chiefs of the Saulteaux. Saskatchewan Archives Board

The Elders have taken the position that treaty rights, obligations, duties, and relationships cannot be determined solely by reference to the written articles of treaty. The Elders observed that those written terms do not adequately reflect the spirit and intent of the treaties nor the outcomes of the original treaty negotiations. They further point out that some of the written terms distort or misrepresent the understandings arrived at treaty and that the so-called official documents include written terms that were not discussed with First Nations at the time the treaties were concluded.

First Nations have taken the position that, in order to arrive at a true understanding of the treaties, the following sources of information must be examined:

1. oral evidence and oral history of Treaty First Nations,
2. Treaty Commissioners reports, writings, and documents;
3. records of missionaries, NWMP, and other eyewitnesses who accompanied the treaty parties along with other relevant historical information, and
4. the so-called articles of treaty.

Many of the provincial governments in Canada and the federal government continue to rely almost exclusively on the written articles of treaty to determine the contents of Indian treaties.

In recent years, the Canadian judiciary has had occasion to consider the approaches that should be used in arriving at an understanding of the historic treaties in Canada. The Supreme Court of Canada has identified the following guidelines that ought to be followed in the interpretation and definition of Indian treaties:

1. Indian treaties should be given a fair, large and liberal construction in favour of Indians.[107]
2. Indian treaties "must ... be construed, not according to the technical meaning of their words ... but in the sense in which they would naturally be understood by the Indians."[108]
3. If there is evidence by conduct or otherwise as to how the parties understood the terms of the treaty, then such understanding and practice is of assistance in giving content to the term or terms.[109]
4. When considering a treaty, a court must take into account the context in which the treaties were negotiated, concluded, and committed to writing. The treaties, as written documents, recorded an agreement that had already been reached orally and they did not always record the full extent of the oral agreement. The treaties were drafted in English by representatives of the Canadian government who, it should be assumed, were familiar with common-law doctrines. Yet, the treaties were not translated in written form into the languages of the various Indian nations who were signatories. Even if they had been, it is unlikely that the Indians, who had a history of

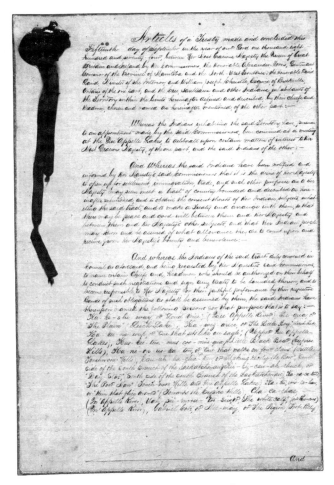

Treaty 4 written manuscript.
National Archives of Canada

TREATY No. 5

BETWEEN

HER MAJESTY THE QUEEN

AND THE

SAULTEAUX AND SWAMPY CREE
TRIBES OF INDIANS

AT

BEREN'S RIVER AND NORWAY HOUSE
WITH ADHESIONS

©
The Queen's Printer, Ottawa, 1969

Cat. No.: R33-0557

IAND Publication No. QS-0573-000-EE-A-1

Treaty 5 Queen's Printer document

communicating only orally, would have understood them any differently. As a result, it is well settled that words in the treaty must not be interpreted in their strict technical sense nor subjected to rigid modern rules of construction.[110]

5. Notwithstanding the challenges created by the use of oral histories as proof of historical facts, the laws of evidence must be adapted in order that this type of evidence can be accommodated and placed on an equal footing with the types of historical evidence that courts are familiar with, which largely consists of historical documents.[111]

6. Where a treaty was concluded verbally and afterwards written up by representatives of the Crown, it would be unconscionable for the Crown to ignore the oral terms while relying on the written terms.[112]

7. The honour of the Crown is always at stake in its dealings with Indian people. Interpretations of treaties and statutory provisions which have an impact upon treaty or aboriginal rights must be approached in a manner which maintains the integrity of the Crown. It is always assumed that the Crown intends to fulfill its promises. No appearance of "sharp dealing" will be sanctioned.[113]

8. It must be remembered that a treaty represents an exchange of solemn promises between the Crown and various Indian Nations. It is an agreement whose nature is sacred.[114]

The Supreme Court of Canada described Indian treaties in the following way:

> In Simon, this Court noted that a treaty with the Indians is unique, that it is an agreement sui generis which is neither created nor terminated according to the rules of international law.[115]

Throughout history, treaties were, and continue to be, instruments through which nations

Open Creek at Neekaneet First Nation

© *Darrell Seib*

establish or regulate relationships with one another. The practice of nations using treaties to regulate their relationships was not unique to European nations. It was an established practice used by nations throughout the world. In North America, prior to the coming of Europeans, Indian nations entered into treaty relationships with one another.

For example, the Cree and Blackfoot-speaking nations entered into a peace treaty with one another to end the hostilities between them. This treaty is known in Cree as "*wîtaskêwin*," meaning an agreement to live together in peace. It should therefore come as no surprise that First Nations languages contained their own definitions of treaty.

Cree Elders use the following phrases to describe the treaties establishing First Nations relationships with European nations: "*itêyimikosiwiyêcikêwina*" (arrangements ordained or inspired by our Father [Creator]).[116]

The arrangements are so described in the Cree language because they originate from Cree teachings and beliefs. They are grounded in the laws of *miyo-wîcêhtowin* governing the manner in which relationships are to be conducted internally among the members of the Cree Nation and externally with other peoples. According to the Elders, the treaties with European nations were made in accordance with these Cree beliefs.

Another phrase used by Cree Elders to describe the treaties with the European nations is "*Okimâw miyo-wîcihitowiyêcikêwin*."[117] This phrase is translated as follows: "agreements or arrangements establishing and organizing good relations or relations of friendship between sovereigns."

As well, in describing treaties, the Elders use the phrase: "*wîtaskê-osihcikêwin*," which means "an agreement or arrangement to live together in peace and harmony."[118]

"*Tipahamâtowin*" is another phrase used by Cree Elders to describe a treaty.[119] It means "treating each other commensurately." At a more formal level, this term describes an act that has been taken where the parties or persons

C. D. Anderson, courtesy of Ted Whitecalf

Image from Diocese of Qu'Appelle; courtesy of the Anglican Church of Canada, General Synod

involved fulfill their mutual and reciprocal undertakings, duties, or responsibilities to one another.

The Elders' teachings and analysis of the treaty relationship with the Crown is conducted within the context of the spiritual traditions of the First Nations. It consequently involves reference to each First Nation's particular conceptual framework and understanding of the relationship between the Creator, his children, and all elements of His Creation.

Hence, in this context, the Elders utilize the knowledge, teachings, laws, doctrines, and values as symbolically represented in part by the following: sun, grass, river, rock, sweetgrass, and pipe stem.

It is clear that, prior to the conclusion of the numbered treaties, which were preceded by a 200-year plus European exposure to Indian nations, Crown representatives were well aware of the spiritual conceptual framework used by Indian Nations and the significance attached to the symbols used by them.

That the Crown was aware of the importance attached to these symbols by the First Nations is clear when one studies the engravings contained in the treaty medals presented at treaty.

The Crown's understanding of the symbolism used by the First Nations at the time the treaties were negotiated is reflected as well by the words written in the purported documents of these treaties: "As long as the sun shines, the rivers flow and the grass grows."

Conversely, in the 200-year plus exposure to Europeans by the Indian nations prior to the signing of treaties, Indian nations as well had developed an understanding of the ways in which symbolism was used by the Crown. At the treaty negotiations, Crown representatives used symbolism in a calculated manner making sure that it was clearly, plainly visible to the Indian nations.

The Elders as well use these symbols to augment their understanding of the treaty relationship and to teach about the character and nature of that relationship. In the context of the relationship of peace and friendship agreed to by treaty between the Indian nations and the Crown, the Elders through symbols used by the Crown during treaty negotiations were of the understanding that the Crown would make available the institutions represented by the symbols it used to augment and complement – not displace – the powers and authorities exercised by the Indian nations and their respective institutions. From the Elders' perspective, the symbols used by each of the treaty parties were meant to symbolize the commitment of each of the parties to maintaining, nurturing, and protecting the relationship of peace, friendship, and alliance agreed to between the nations who were party to the treaties.

One of the major impediments to reaching a mutually acceptable understanding of treaties between Canadian governments and First Nations arises from the continuing insistence of Crown legal advisors that the content and meaning of Indian treaties be determined primarily, if not exclusively, from the written texts of treaties or the so-called articles of treaties.

Chipewyans who accepted Treaty No. 8 at Fond du Lac, 1899. Left to right: Toussaint, Chief Moberley, and Laurent Dzieddin. Glenbow Archives

Emil Gardipy, Beardy's and Okemasis First Nation

© *Ted Whitecalf*

In part, this approach is dictated by the way in which some laws are structured with respect to those matters that are deemed to be official records of the government or the Crown.

Under Canadian law, a document published by the Queen's Printer is deemed to be the official record of a document. Unless and until proof is provided that such a document cannot be relied upon, it remains almost the sole basis for determining its validity and its contents.

Until recently, this law, combined with evidentiary laws governing legal proceedings, made the written text of treaties the primary, if not at times the exclusive, source for determining the content of Indian treaties.

Though recent case law (referred to earlier) has altered the evidentiary rules with respect to historic treaties, there is yet to be any alteration to the laws governing what constitutes official transcripts or records insofar as the Indian treaties are concerned.

Though the issue of determining the contents of the Indian treaties has been recognized and extensively commented upon, Canada and the First Nations have yet to address how the problem is to be resolved. While awaiting resolution, the current situation continues to give rise to sharply conflicting views of the purposes served by these treaties and the rights either recognized, affirmed, or granted through the formal agreements of the sovereign Indian First Nations and the British Crown.

The difficulties associated with the situation were noted in 1983 by a special parliamentary committee report on Indian self-government in Canada:

> Indian people view treaties as reaffirmations of their sovereignty and rights as agreements to allow settlements in certain areas; non-Indians regard treaties as an extinguishment of rights, an acceptance of the supremacy of the Crown, and a generous gift of land to the Indians so that they might have land of their own.[120]

The Elders' presentations dealing with *wîtaskêwin* (living together on the land) and *pimâcihowin* (making a living) directly contradict the written texts of the treaties in Saskatchewan and past case law predicated on those written texts. They do so in the following ways:

The traditional First Nations view of treaties has been that they are agreements negotiated between the British Crown and sovereign First Nations. The issue of sovereign treaty-making capacity remains unresolved in part because there is continuing unwillingness on the part of Canada to acknowledge that First Nations possessed sovereign capacity when they negotiated the treaties with the British Crown.

On the question of original sovereign title of First Nations traditional lands and territories, the government of Canada claims that the Crown has underlying sovereign title. The Elders maintain the position that First Nations were given the land by the Creator and hence were given original sovereign title, possession, and ownership of their lands and territories.

© Tourism Saskatchewan

Cree Chief Starblanket (born c. 1832). His people came into Treaty 4 on September 15, 1874, with Starblanket's father White Calf (Wa pii Moos Toosis), his mother was Piyesis (The Bird). Starblanket took over leadership from his father the year after they entered treaty and remained in the position until 1917. Morris Collection, Provincial Archives of Manitoba

On the question as to whether "Indian title" was extinguished by Treaties 4, 5, 6, 8, and 10, the government of Canada claims First Nations did: "cede, release, surrender and yield up to the government of the Dominion of Canada for Her Majesty the Queen and her successors forever, all their rights, titles, and privileges whatsoever to the lands."

The Elders maintained that such extinguishment was never agreed to by First Nations during treaty negotiations. At the focus sessions, when the "extinguishment clauses" of the written treaty texts were read, translated, and explained, the Elders reacted with incredulity and disbelief. They found it hard to believe that anyone, much less the Crown, could seriously believe that First Nations would ever have agreed to "extinguish" their God-given rights.

The Elders believe that they never gave up their territorial rights as they are defined by the concepts of *wîtaskêwin* and *pimâcihowin* – these rights are fundamental and integral to the treaty relationship and in fact stand at variance with the written texts of the treaties in Saskatchewan.

The Crown asserts exclusive ownership and jurisdiction over all lands, wildlife, and resources. The Elders state that the First Nations retained ownership and jurisdiction over all lands, wildlife, and resources, except for those portions required for agricultural purposes – which were to be shared to the depth of a plough blade.

Fundamental contradictions exist between First Nations oral history and understanding of the treaties and the written text of Treaties 4, 5, 6, 8, and 10. The result is that there is as yet no mutually agreed upon text or record of the treaties in existence.

The 1996 *Report of the Royal Commission on Aboriginal Peoples* made the following recommendations as a basis for resolving or addressing these issues. It recommends that Canada change its basic presumptions as follows:

There is a presumption in respect of the historical treaties that:

- treaty nations did not intend to consent to the blanket extinguishment of their Aboriginal rights and title by entering into the treaty relationship;
- treaty nations intended to share the territory and jurisdiction and management over it, as opposed to ceding the territory, even where the text of an historical treaty makes reference to a blanket extinguishment of land rights; and
- treaty nations did not intend to give up their inherent right of governance by entering into a treaty relationship, and the act of treaty making is regarded as an affirmation rather than a denial of that right.[121]

Until the parties can agree on a process for reconciling these fundamentally contradicting records of the treaties, it will be difficult for them to create the partnership and reconciliation that both desire.

While, on the one hand, the fundamental variance between the oral and written record of the treaties might be seen as questioning the validity of the treaties, the Elders are adamant about the fact that such is not the case.

Indeed, in a number different areas, the written texts and First Nations oral history indicate that the parties reached substantive agreements at the treaty negotiations. It is clear that the treaty parties intended to create peaceful relations among each other, that they desired to "live together" and they desired to share in the livelihood opportunities arising from the land.

For the Elders, what is at issue is not whether or not treaties exist, but whether a mutually acceptable record of them can now be agreed upon and implemented. They remain confident that if the fundamental values identified by them guide any future process and if *tâpwêwin* (truth) is the basis for arriving at an agreement on a mutually acceptable record of the treaties, the parties, with good faith, ought to be able to succeed in reaching such an agreement.

Treaty party, Fond du Lac, Saskatchewan, c. 1903-06. Treaty 8. Sgt. Fitzgerald, NWMP, on extreme left. Also included are Dr. Edwards, H.A. Conroy, and J. Edmonton. Glenbow Archives

Askîwipimâcihowascikêwina
Setting into Place Arrangements for Livelihood, Living and Evolving Treaty Rights

Elder John James Head, Red Earth First Nation, Treaty 5

Elder Joe Crowe, Kahkewistahaw First Nation, Treaty 4

"*Askîwipimâcihowascikêwina*" is a Cree phrase that speaks to the livelihood arrangements discussed at treaty negotiations. The term "*askiy*," meaning "earth, or land," is used to distinguish those things that have to do with life here on earth or the land and those things that have to do with matters affecting the soul or the spirit.

The Elders in the previous chapters discussed those aspects of the treaty negotiations that had to do with enduring principles that operate outside the constraints of time, timeless values, or principles that serve as a guide to successive generations and will continue to be ready to serve those yet unborn.

The Elders as well focussed a lot of attention on those matters that speak to the material needs of their people and those things that need to be addressed if their people are to be able to participate in the contemporary blessings that their lands and territories continue to generate.

As discussed earlier, both the written and oral versions of the treaties speak to the treaty guarantee and protection of livelihood (*pimâcihowin*), promised to First Nations and their peoples.

From the understanding of First Nations, treaty was made to ensure that their way of life would not change – to protect them from potential intrusion from outsiders. But has that way of life been really protected? Alfred Billette from the Buffalo River Dene Nation has experienced encroachment of outsiders that has dramatically altered his ability to carry on with his way of life:

> When I was young, I remember trapping and hunting with people in the Primrose Lake area west of Dillon. We were free to do what we wanted within our traditional hunting areas. That changed in the 1950s when the military took that land from us and changed it into a restricted area to be used for the sole purpose of military exercises. I believe that's a direct infringement on my treaty rights. Now, we can't even hunt there without fearing serious charges. Some of our hunters were charged recently for hunting in the range. We beat the government on those charges, but now we're back in court because the government has appealed them. What happened to the treaty when it was supposed to protect us? Nobody has a right to break the treaty promises. I don't want to see any more encroachment by anyone over our traditional territories![122]

"Way of Life" or Ways of Making a Living

The treaties uniformly guaranteed the First Nations that their "way of life" would be unaffected. "Way of life" can be understood in different ways. It can be understood to mean that the "way in which people lived" would remain unchanged and unaffected. Hence some might say that "way of life" meant that, forever into the future, Indians would be "free to hunt, trap, and fish" for a livelihood. Considering the context of the times during which the treaties were negotiated, some might be excused if they believed that First Nations were content and satisfied with a promise that their way of life would be forever frozen in time.

However understandable that viewpoint might be, it would totally misconstrue the intentions of the First Nations parties to treaty. It is true that they wanted to (and, in their view, did) achieve a guarantee that they would continue to be important participants in the economic environment as it was then. But they looked beyond the present as it was then and tried to fashion agreements that would endure the test of time. That is why they concentrated on securing "livelihood" arrangements or guarantees through treaty.

Liberty, freedom, independence, and economic self-sufficiency were the goals they sought to achieve for those were values that were central and integral to their way of life. Through their traditions and teachings, First Nations learned early in their existence that, without *pimâcihisowin* (the ability to make one's living), *tipêyimisowin* (freedom, or liberty), and *tipiyawâtisowin* (independence), they and their peoples could not survive. And indeed for the 200-year period prior to treaties, they had entered into "living arrangements" with the White man that enabled them to continue living their way of

life – and their way of life meant that, through economic self-sufficiency, they were able to continue living in freedom, independence, and liberty. That, from a First Nations perspective, is what was and is meant by "way of life."

In this chapter, the Elders speak of the means that were promised to guarantee and protect the economic well-being of First Nations and their peoples. They derive their understanding from both the recollection of the treaty negotiations and their concepts of *wîtaskêwin* and *pimâcihowin* – concepts that were and continue to be integral to their traditional and cultural beliefs. They understood that the Crown promised to provide the means to enable or encourage First Nations and their peoples either to continue with their traditional modes of livelihood or to enter into new ways of livelihood that would accompany the arrival of White settlers to their territories.

Elder Norbert Fern, Fond du Lac Denesuline Nation, Treaty 8

Courtesy Northern Resources Trucking and F-11 Photographic Design

Chief Piapot. A prominent chief during the treaty negotiations, he demanded that the treaty document specifically include provision for farm instructors, mills, forges, mechanics, more tools and machinery, and medical assistance.
Saskatchewan Archives Board

The Elders believed that each of the parties to the treaties wanted to provide the basis upon which their respective peoples would be afforded the opportunity to benefit and grow from the wealth that would be created by their treaty relationship and their agreement to share the land.

The Elders' understanding of the treaty negotiations is reflected in the Report submitted by the Commissioners of Treaty No. 8.

Treaty Land-Sharing Arrangements

Treaty 8 Commissioners' Report:

> Indeed, the Indians were generally averse to being placed on reserve.
>
> It would have been impossible to have made a treaty with them if we had not assured them that there was no intention of confining them to reserves.
>
> We had to clearly explain to them that the provision for reserves and allotments of land were made for their protection, and to secure to them in perpetuity A FAIR PORTION of the land ceded, in the event of settlement advancing.[123]

First Nations Understanding:

The Elders state that the principle underlying the treaty land-sharing would be to provide an equitable land base to the treaty signatories.

Sharing would be to provide an equitable land base from which White and First Nations peoples would derive a livelihood.

The Elders from the different First Nations – Cree, Saulteaux, Assiniboine, and Dene – participating in separate meetings held within each their treaty areas were unequivocal, and remarkably consistent throughout the province, when describing the nature and character of the land-sharing arrangements agreed to by the First Nations during the treaty negotiations.

Elder Danny Musqua (Treaty 4) said:

> Because, if any man owns a piece of the Earth, then he no more respects Mother Earth. He no more respects the Earth, because he believes he can do what he wants with that Earth and he can destroy it, he can do whatever he wants. That's the reason why we don't own the Earth, because it belongs to all the people. For the purposes of that we cannot own the Earth. We were willing to share it.[124]

* * *

First, the Elders asserted, clearly and unequivocally that the treaties were not a total blanket transfer of First Nations lands and territories to the Crown.

Elder Kay Thompson (Treaty 4) said:

> They didn't give the land, they didn't say, we give you this land. They just gave them permission to use the land. That's how I used to hear them talk a long time ago. Another thing I don't like in the reports [of the Commissioner and Indian Affairs] is that Indians surrendered their land; they didn't surrender their land and I don't go for that because I hear different on the Indian side. This land is ours. That's what I always hear old people saying long ago. We never gave it up; we never surrendered anything, but I hear that today on the White man's side, surrendered, lands surrendered. That's the agents that are saying that. They

reported that, Indians surrendered land. The Indians did not surrender land.[125]

Second, the Elders stated that the land-sharing arrangements agreed to by the First Nations were limited to those lands required for agricultural purposes.

Elder Gordon Oakes (Treaty 4) said:

> The words that I am going to say are not from the treaty book. I got this information from the Elder in the early forties. He was listening at the time they negotiated the treaties; this is where I am going to get my words ... as far as I concerned the treaties, they are not finished yet. They are not finished, like the 1930 transfer agreement that should never take place, because we only gave a tip of a plough at this country....
>
> Treaty 4 alone I am talking about; we surrendered 75,000 miles, square miles on Treaty 4; a tip of a plough, that's what we negotiated. There were two nations that negotiated the treaty. You know, this country belongs to the Indian people; the Creator gave us this country. Then the treaties were taking place, that's what they gave up, a tip of a plough, so the people that come from elsewhere, different countries, they can farm, ranch, all that. We never gave up anything more than that.[126]

Elder Jimmy Myo (Treaty 6) said:

> We got no business to give it up, we got no business to sell that land. We got no business to lease that land. We got no business to make any kind of deal on that land, but when the White man came to make a deal with us, the old people knew that we could try to treat them like our own relatives, so that they could use that land at the certain amount of ... like Gordon

[Oakes] said, the depth of the plough. That was the only part that they let them use. Other than that, below the depth of a plough was supposed to be negotiated after like he said, but it never was; they never did negotiate that right up to date they haven't done anything. That's why we hear our Elders keep on saying we didn't let the White man take more than this much. That's about six inches, the depth of a plough. We did not give up the land, we did not sell the land. Those are the things that was told to us, by the Elders never to say: we sold, we lease, we give up, anything like that.[127]

Third, the Elders asserted that the First Nations did not, through treaty, share the natural resources – either renewable or non-renewable, surface or subsurface – located on their respective territories with the Crown. These the First Nations retained for themselves.

Elder Kay Thompson (Treaty 4) said:

> All these things were made in such a way that they can't give up that land. They can't say, promise you this and then go back on their word. On land especially, the land was something the [Indians] never wanted to part with, Indians never wanted to part with their land. It was given to them from above. This was our country. They always said that. This is our country. We are free to live anywhere, and we are free to live any place. I never hear them say, I gave this country to them, I surrender, I never hear that.[128]

Elder Gordon Oakes (Treaty 4) said:

> The Natural Resources Transfer Agreement of 1930 should never have happened. The result of that is now that the province owns all the mines and minerals. I worked on land

Dene chief who had come to Lac La Ronge where "Treaty" was being paid. Saskatchewan Archives Board

© Ted Whitecalf

claims for many years and now we have concluded our claim. This is where I had difficulty in our negotiations was with respect to minerals. The province claims that he owns, but where did he get it from? These, my relatives, we have to make good or correct.[129]

Fourth, the Elders asserted that the First Nations did not share, through the treaties, the water resources located on their territory with the Crown, except for amounts required for domestic agricultural purposes by the agricultural settlers.

Elder Gordon Oakes (Treaty 4) said:

We were given this by our Creator and now the White man takes these riches right from our hands, right from the palm of our hands. In the meantime, many social ills continue. Mines and minerals were given up; water was given up; water was given up only from wells for farming purposes and domestic use.[130]

Fifth, the Elders asserted that the First Nations did not, by treaty, share the wildlife, waterfowl, or fish with the Crown. These, the First Nations retained for their exclusive use.

Senator Allan Bird (Treaty 6) said:

For those of us who are up north, we're not involved in agriculture too much but nevertheless were still promised, we were promised to hunt, to gather, to live off the land. At that time, the government said that we would live together, that I am not here to take away what you have now.[131]

Elder August Lidguerre (Treaty 8) said:

The animals, the wildlife is here for us; the Creator put it here for us. No government can own that.[132]

Elder Norbert Fern (Treaty 8) said:

With relation to fishing, hunting, and trapping, I just want to add to that, that was our way. Our way of the people. When treaties were signed, people lived like that....

It is our land. It is our lake ... we need to provide for our families. We need to do the best that we can for our families through the lake.[133]

Elder Joe Crowe (Treaty 4) said:

We have no business giving up the land that the Creator owns, the trees, all those things, I'm repeating those again just to make myself feel good. Again, I could speak lots about treaties because those old Elders talked to me, talked to me, and then eventually I get a grasp of it. That's from 1954 right into 1955 and so they still kept after me. Don't go this way; don't go that way; just stay with the Indian way; don't add on or subtract; just follow the teachings.[134]

The Elders made clear that all the matters referred to above were conferred by the Creator upon the Indian Nations and, until shared by them, belong exclusively to the First Nations.

Elder John James Mercredi (Treaty 8) said:

There are a lot of people that came from across the big water, and you have to remember too that they are newcomers, and we, the people, the First Nations people who live here, are the First Peoples of Canada. When you came here, when your relatives came here a long time ago, we welcomed them. We are not even respected or recognized within our traditional homelands. Our rights, our ways, were always basically people blocking us, trying to get in our way. Trying to divert our attention so that we lose ways and our land. We talk about our land, nothing else. And we don't block anyone else from coming and sharing our land with us.[135]

The issue of the Hudson's Bay transfer of Rupert's Land to the Crown in 1870 was identified as an item raised but not resolved during the Treaty 4 negotiations and which now needs to be addressed.

Elder Danny Musqua (Treaty 4) said:

There was a land acquisition deal that had just taken place without the full knowledge or the agreement of the nations that were there who owned the land. And that was Prince Rupert's Territory, which the Crown had paid 300,000 [pounds sterling] to Prince Rupert for his claim of that land, which gave him title to that land [*sic*]. How can you get title when you don't even own the land? Or how can you even ascertain the right to sell that land when you didn't even have the agreement with the First Nations that were there to get that land. This was one of the big issues that was in the way, and if you read the documents of Treaty 4 you will see that was very much a very impending problem for Treaty 4. The way the Commissioner went around that and again you will not find it in your documentary, you will not find it in the Morris Book of treaties, he makes a statement because he wasn't getting anywhere with these people. They weren't willing to talk; they weren't going to begin to convey any meaningful transition of agreements, until this 300,000 [pounds] was specifically identified as to who had the legal right to receive it. We can't talk about this because somebody else owns this land already.

There's a man who is a king from across the ocean who apparently owns this land, and he has the right to sell it…. Where did he get an agreement from these people to actually sell that land back to the Crown? We need to understand that they weren't redundantly ignorant, they just wanted an understanding from the Commissioner. Look, you have to tell us how this man was able to sell that. Under what authority did he have the right to sell that land to the Crown? And under what right did the Crown have the authority or the right to buy

Andrew Arcand (left) and Terrence Gladue. Courtesy of Saskatchewan Indian Institute of Technologies

Chief White Cap of the Cree band located just east of Batoche. During the 1885 Resistance, some of his men were forced to fight with the Métis at Batoche. Even though they fought against their will, they were persecuted by the government for many years afterwards for what was perceived as disloyalty. Glenbow Archives

that land of him, when they are just going to make a deal with us now to get some kind of agreement on the use of that?[136]

Wîtaskêwin, as explained by the Elders, meant no more than an initial land-sharing arrangement to allow the Crown's subjects to derive an agricultural livelihood from First Nations territories.

With respect to the issue of future territorial sharing arrangements for other purposes, the initial treaty process was to provide a framework within which further arrangements arising from the agreement to live together was to be discussed in subsequent treaty negotiations between the treaty parties.

Elder Danny Musqua said:

> We agreed to the relationship, a perpetual land-use agreement between us [First Nations] and them [the Crown] in Treaty 4, that [settlers] would harvest the land for the purposes of agriculture, sow crops and we, along with that, [would learn agricultural skills]; they would give us the technology to also do that ourselves.[137]

With respect to land-sharing arrangements, the Elders' understanding was that the initial treaty discussions focussed solely on the agricultural land requirements of the Crown, which would be used by her British subjects. To the extent required by the Crown, though without jeopardy to their own emerging requirements in this area, the First Nations agreed to share some of their lands with the Crown for these purposes.

We did not, in the preliminary round, explore the quantitative aspect of these arrange-

ments in terms of trying to determine what portions of First Nations territories were retained or shared for agricultural purposes. This matter will have to be examined in the future.

What we can say at this point is that, given the nature of the treaty relationship based on *wîtaskêwin* (living together on the land), and *pimâcihowin* (making a living), the sharing arrangements, as envisioned by the Elders, were to be fair to each of the parties, intended to enable the parties to jointly share in the prosperity of the land – not drive the First Nations to destitution.

Elder Kay Thompson said:

> How are we going to survive because a lot of our people are not working, they're not employed, they're on welfare, they'd like to work but ... sometimes when they go out they're turned down because ... they're Indian. So they're just on the reserve and when they take welfare, they don't like to take it because when they go out, the way that they get harassed about welfare, just laying around doing nothing, you lazy Indians. Things like that are being said and they're being hurt. But what could they do, what else could they do when they're unemployed and they go for work and they get turned down. A lot of issues like that are hurting our people.[138]

The state of dependence created by unemployment or the inability to work (*atoskêwin*) is a source of continuing deep anxiety for the Elders. During these sessions, they focussed on the land-sharing arrangements arising from treaty as a basis upon which the economic and social needs of their people can and ought to be addressed. For them, the land base of First Nations must be adequate if they are to overcome the social and economic difficulties that they now face. The Elders cannot see how "self-governance" is going to be viable unless it is implemented on the land-sharing principles contemplated by First Nations at the time treaty was signed. They spoke at length of the wealth that their traditional territories generate without any direct benefit to their peoples. They believe that proper sharing of those resources would generate the revenue base that their governments require and provide once again economic self-sufficiency to their peoples.

They addressed the need as well for the parties to examine those treaty promises pertaining to "the means" or ways in which their people should receive the assistance promised by the Crown during treaty. The Elders indicated their clear understanding that the treaty promised that First Nations would receive required assistance to enable them to participate in economic times and environments as they changed in the future. That was, in their view, the treaty guarantee designed to enable their peoples to continue to possess, in the future, the ability to make their own living. They cite as an example the treaty promise to provide "oxen and walking ploughs." In their view, this was a promise that assistance would be provided for those of their people who wanted to "make a living" from the agricultural economy. In their view, the treaties need to be implemented in accordance with changing times such that the

assistance for "making a living" from the agricultural economy should reflect contemporary times and environments.

They discussed education in the context of the economic environment. In their view, the educational rights recognized by treaty were designed to enable First Nations to acquire the capacity required to develop educational facilities and institutions. At the same time, these promises were designed to enable their peoples to "acquire the cunning of the White man" such that they would acquire the skills required to enable them to participate in the new economies that they saw arriving with the Europeans.

Throughout the presentations and the focus meetings, the Elders continued to emphasize and re-emphasize the need to restore the self-sufficiency of First Nations and their peoples. In their view, that could only occur if the parties implement the spirit and intent of their treaties.

Chief Moses Gordon and his wife, Treaty 4. Saskatchewan Archives Board

Conclusion
"... so that they may have a good future"

While we sought, to the best of our abilities, to relate what the Elders have told us about treaties and treaty-making, what we have not done, and what is lacking in this document, are the many stories related at many sessions that described

© Ted Whitecalf

the hardships and burdens that individuals and communities have endured in the era since the treaties were concluded. Often it was older mothers who, through tears, told of their experiences in coping with and working to heal those who were victims of abuse in residential schools. Emotions of frustration, anger, and sadness were related to those of us who sat rivetted by accounts of the horror that so many experienced. Elder Mel Joseph described a younger brother being whipped like a dog, and Elder Isabel McNab told one session of the occasion when she was riding in her nephew's truck and asked him why he was always so angry. The nephew stopped the truck, overcome by emotion, and then told her of the abuse he endured at residential school. Elder McNab told the session that she felt the whole world had gone dark and that the sun wasn't shining any more. Elder McNab spoke eloquently at a number of sessions about her people living in cities whom she referred to as the poorest of the poor. The plight of mothers and children living in destitution and third world conditions weighed heavily on her. Yet, despite her grim descriptions, she remained optimistic about the regeneration of those damaged by abuse and poverty. Elder McNab stated that healing through the guidance of Elders in sweat lodges and other ceremonies remained the most effective means of overcoming physical, emotional, and psychological pain.

Successive generations of Elders have been involved in attempting to clarify the perspectives of First Nations as they relate to treaties and the treaty process. They have consistently emphasized the spiritual beliefs that underlie treaty making, especially on key points of land ownership, land sharing, and the rights handed to them by the Creator to make a living from the land as embodied in the Cree word "*pimâcihowin*." Their points have been made repeatedly in various forums, be it in litigation or parliamentary committees, or various public inquiries such as the Royal Commission on Aboriginal Peoples.

Once again, in Saskatchewan, Elders from many nations, language groups, and areas have participated in a process facilitated by Treaty Commissioner Judge David Arnot about the treaty relationship, their relationship to the land, and their right to earn a living from the land.

Since the 1970s, a consensus has emerged from the work of scholars to show that treaties were not understood by First Nations narrowly, as land surrenders, but were understood as land-sharing agreements that assured First Nations the right to earn a living through continuing traditional ways of earning a living or by adopting new ways such as agriculture. Scholars have clearly documented that First Nations negoti-

ated for and worked to establish a variety of economic promises/clauses that they believed would ensure their right to a livelihood.[139] First Nations understood that the right to make a living was a fundamental part of what was agreed to in the treaties. First Nations not only wanted to work at traditional livelihoods but were anxious to adopt new ones as part of the sharing agreement secured by the treaties. Thus, both in the legal arena and through the historical record, this right to livelihood has been documented and does not differ from what the

© *Tourism Saskatchewan*

Wayway Sasap, chief of one band of the Saulteaux.
Saskatchewan Archives Board

Elders have been saying. The Elders in this process are once again anxious to explain their perspective on the livelihood issue because they believe it is crucial to counteract the negative and damaging stereotypes of the lazy Indian disseminated by non-Aboriginal culture. Much more needs to be done to disseminate the First Nations point of view on livelihood, and indeed the requirement to work, which they believed the treaty process was surely about.

The world view that the Elders described to us is comprehensive and complex. Their doctrines and principles for survival are linked to their Creation stories, where the Creator made an island for them with various peoples being placed throughout the island. The new world was created out of an old world where war and discord prevailed, and the new world was one where principles of peace and harmony between individuals and people were to prevail. The power of the Creator was evident in the powerful forces that surrounded people on earth – the forces of the sun, water, trees, and rocks. Animals, fish, berries, and roots were provided to the First Nations to allow for their survival. There was a central sacredness about the land given the First Nations and also to the spirits of the powerful forces of nature. There was great reverence for the spirit world. First Nations principles and doctrines for life on earth reflected the great respect for Mother Earth and the spirit world. Principles of peace and sharing governed all individual and kinship relations. The central and primary principles of respect for the land then extended to all those

on the land, to family, to relatives, and to other peoples. The new world was to be a place for peace and harmony, and the spiritual principles of living with an attitude of respect for the land and all that was connected to it was expanded to human relations. Central to the First Nations belief systems were sacred ceremonies that gave them access to the Creator and His Creation. First Nations doctrines and principles of peace, harmony, and sharing were established and affirmed through ceremonies where sacred vows were made. The pipe and the circle were paramount in their spiritual practices. The pipe was one of the mediums used to ground the vows made to the Creator.

Thus, there is a connecting linkage from the Creator to the land he gave the First Nations and the peace principles and doctrines, through to the land and respect for Mother Earth. These doctrines and principles also apply to relations between peoples, whether kinship relations or those between peoples, and on to the principles of sharing for survival with the rights and obligations to provide for the survival of all individuals and peoples. Survival was assured to theFirst Nations by the gift of the land and all that was connected to it, and it was up to individuals and nations to pursue livelihoods that would guarantee survival. For the Elders, there is a clear and logical connection between the spiritual principles and doctrines given to them by the Creator through Mother Earth to the material reality of surviving on the land. Thus, there is a spiritual foundation to the concrete need to live in peace on the land. The

Elders have clearly related this to us through their careful and detailed explanations that are connected to concepts such as *miyo-wîcêhtowin* and *wîtaskêwin*.

Historically, non-Aboriginal people have seen and described evidence of the ceremonies that reflect the First Nations spirituality and of their efforts to peacefully co-exist both among themselves and with newcomers. The principles of living with respect for the land and all those that the Creator has put on Earth were evident to newcomers in pipe ceremonies that were used to establish peaceful and harmonious relations, first with fur traders and explorers, then with early colonizers, and finally through the treaties negotiated with the Crown. Throughout their history, the material means for survival were based on a comprehensive and complex spiritual foundation.

It has not been possible to include all the conceptual issues raised by the Elders during this process. Some of the conceptual issues raised will require further detailed examination, study, and analysis, particularly with respect to the evolution and development of institutional relationships between First Nations and the Crown. The concepts described by Elders are often complex and intricate in their own context and are even more difficult to contextualize in a cross-cultural comparative framework.

We wish to reiterate our gratitude for the personal and organizational assistance provided to us by the Federation of Saskatchewan Indian Nations and the Office of the Treaty Commissioner.

Most of all, we thank each and every one of the Elders who made a presentation and apologize to all those whose words or thoughts we did not specifically cite or include.

We are confident, however, that this book, taken as a whole, reflects the thoughts of the Elders. They expressed a strong hope that a strengthening of the treaty relationship can serve as the basis for securing a lasting, productive, and healthy place for First Nations and their peoples in the treaty partnership with the Crown, Her governments, and Her citizens.

As Senator Allan Bird has said:

> We are here for a very important reason; it is for our grandchildren so that they may have a good future.[140]

Indian men harvesting with binders on Assiniboine reserve near Wolsely, 1900-01. Saskatchewan Archives Board

Notes

1. Elder Jimmy Myo (Moosomin First Nation, Treaty 6), August 19, 1997, FSIN Elders meeting, Wanuskewin Heritage Park, Saskatoon. This was reaffirmed throughout meetings with Elders and reiterated by FSIN Senators and Elders who attended an Elders Focus Session in Saskatoon on March 22, 1999.

2. Elder Peter Waskahat (Frog Lake First Nation, Treaty 6), November 16, 1997, FSIN Elders Focus Session, Saskatoon, Saskatchewan. Translated from Cree.

3. Elder Norman Sunchild (Thunderchild First Nation, Treaty 6), November 12, 1997, Treaty Elders Forum, Jackfish Lake Lodge, Cochin, Saskatchewan. Translated from Cree.

4. Elder Kay Thompson (Carry the Kettle First Nation, Treaty 4), January 12, 1998, FSIN Elders Focus Session, Saskatoon, Saskatchewan.

5. *St. Catherine's Milling and Lumber Co.* v. *The Queen* (1885), 10 O.R. 196 (Chancery) at 206.

6. *Delgamuukw v. British Columbia*, [1998] 1 C.N.L.R. 14, (S.C.C.), reversing in part, [1993] 5 C.N.L.R., [1993] 5 W.W.R. 97 (B.C.C.A.), varying in part [1991] 5 C.N.L.R., [1991], 79 D.L.R. (4th) 185 (B.C.S.C.).

7. *Delgamuukw v. British Columbia*, 79 D.L.R. (4th) 185 (B.C.S.C.). McEachern, C.J.B.C.

8. Elder Jacob Bill (Pelican Lake First Nation, Treaty 6), December 13, 1997, FSIN Elders Focus Session, Saskatoon, Saskatchewan. Translated from Cree.

9. Elder Dolly Neapetung (Yellow Quill First Nation, Treaty 4), September 15, 1997, Treaty Elders Forum, Fort Qu'Appelle and Wapii-Moostoosis Reserve, Lebret, Saskatchewan. Translated from Saulteaux.

10. Elder Bart McDonald (Fond du Lac Denesuline Nation, Treaty 8), November 5, 1997, Treaty Elders Forum, Fond du Lac, Saskatchewan. Translated from Dene.

11. Victor Echodh (Acting Chief, Black Lake Denesuline Nation, Treaty 8), November 4, 1997, Treaty Elders Forum, Black Lake, Saskatchewan. Translated from Dene.

12. Elder Peter Waskahat (Frog Lake First Nation, Treaty 6), November 15-16, 1997, FSIN Elders Focus Session, Saskatoon, Saskatchewan. Translated from Cree.

13. Elder Kay Thompson (Carry the Kettle First Nation, Treaty 4), May 14, 1997, FSIN Indian Child & Family Services interview.

14. Victor Echodh (Acting Chief, Black Lake Denesuline Nation, Treaty 8), November 4, 1997, Treaty Elders Forum, Black Lake, Saskatchewan. Translated from Dene.

15. Elder Dolly Neapetung (Yellow Quill First Nation, Treaty 4), September 15, 1997, Treaty Elders Forum, Wapii-Moostoosis Reserve, Lebret, Saskatchewan. Translated from Saulteaux.

16. Elder Norman Sunchild (Thunderchild First Nation, Treaty 6), November 12, 1997, Treaty Elders Forum, Jackfish Lake Lodge, Cochin, Saskatchewan. Translated from Cree.

17. Elder Jacob Bill (Pelican Lake First Nation, Treaty 6), November 12, 1997, Treaty Elders Forum, Jackfish Lake Lodge, Cochin, Saskatchewan. Translated from Cree.

18. Elder Jacob Bill (Pelican Lake First Nation, Treaty 6), April 30, 1997, FSIN Senate Meeting, Jackfish Lake Lodge, Cochin, Saskatchewan. Translated from Cree.

19. Elder Jimmy Myo (Moosomin First Nation, Treaty 6), May 22-23, 1997, Treaty Elders Forum, Nekaneet First Nation, Maple Creek, Saskatchewan.

20. Elder Jacob Bill (Pelican Lake First Nation, Treaty 6), April 30, 1997, FSIN Senate Meeting, Jackfish Lake Lodge, Cochin, Saskatchewan. Translated from Cree.

21 Elder Lawrence Tobacco (Kawacatoose First Nation, Treaty 4), September 14, 1997, Treaty Elders Forum, Wapii-Moostoosis Reserve, Lebret, Saskatchewan.

22 Elder Peter Waskahat (Frog Lake First Nation, Treaty 6), November 15, 1997, FSIN Elders Focus Session, Saskatoon, Saskatchewan. Translated from Cree.

23 Elder Norman Sunchild (Thunderchild First Nation, Treaty 6), November 12, 1997, Treaty Elders Forum, Jackfish Lake Lodge, Cochin, Saskatchewan. Translated from Cree.

24 Elder Peter Waskahat (Frog Lake First Nation, Treaty 6), November 15, 1997, Treaty Elders Forum, Jackfish Lake Lodge, Cochin, Saskatchewan. Translated from Cree.

25 Elder Isabel McNab (Gordon's First Nation, Treaty 4), September 15, 1997, Treaty Elders Forum, Wapii-Moostoosis Reserve, Lebret, Saskatchewan.

26 Elder Jacob Bill (Pelican Lake First Nation, Treaty 6), November 14-15, 1997, FSIN Elders Focus Session, Saskatoon, Saskatchewan. Translated from Cree.

27 Senator Frank McIntyre (English River First Nation, Treaty 10), August 7, 1997, FSIN Elders Meeting, Wanuskewin Heritage Park, Saskatoon, Saskatchewan.

28 Elder Peter Waskahat (Frog Lake First Nation, Treaty 6), November 15-16, 1997, FSIN Elders Focus Session, Saskatoon, Saskatchewan. Translated from Cree.

29 Morris, Alexander, *The Treaties of Canada with The Indians of Manitoba and the North-West Territories including the Negotiations on which they were based* (Toronto: Belfords, Clarke, 1880), p. 296.

30 The term for "Creator" in Nakoda (Assiniboine) is *Adaylua Wahkantanga*; in Cree, the word used is *wiyohtawimaw*; in Dene, the word used is *yedariyé*. The Ojibway/Saulteaux term for "Great Spirit" is *Kihci-Manito*.

31 Elder Pauline Mercredi (Fond du Lac Denesuline Nation, Treaty 8), November 5, 1997, Treaty Elders Forum, Fond du Lac, Saskatchewan. Translated from Dene.

32 Elder Celeste Randhill (Fond du Lac Denesuline Nation, Treaty 8) November 5, 1997, Treaty Elders Forum, Fond du Lac, Saskatchewan.

33 Elder Isabel McNab (Gordon First Nation, Treaty 4), September 15, 1997, Treaty Elders Forum, Wapii-Moostoosis Reserve, Lebret, Saskatchewan.

34 Elder Dolly Neapetung (Yellow Quill First Nation, Treaty 4), September 14-15, 1997, Treaty Elders Forum, Fort Qu'Appelle and Wapii-Moostoosis Reserve, Lebret, Saskatchewan. Translated from Saulteaux.

35 Elder Kay Thompson (Carry the Kettle First Nation, Treaty 4), May 14, 1997, FSIN Indian Child and Family Services interview.

36 Elder Alma Kytwayhat (Makwa Sahgaiehcan First Nation, Treaty 6), December 21, 1997, FSIN interview, Saskatoon, Saskatchewan. Interview and translation from Cree by Albert Angus.

37 *St. Catherines Milling Co.* v. *The Queen* (1885), 10 O.R. 196 (Chancery), at 228.

38 Elder Alfred Billette (Buffalo River Denesuline Nation, Treaty 10), March 28, 2000, FSIN Elders Focus Session, Saskatoon, Saskatchewan. Translated from Dene.

39 Elder Gordon Oakes (Nekaneet First Nation, Treaty 4), August 6, 1997, FSIN Elders meeting, Wanuskewin Heritage Park, Saskatoon, Saskatchewan.

40 Elder Simon Kytwayhat (Makwa Sahgaiehcan First Nation, Treaty 6), December 21, 1997, FSIN interview, Saskatoon, Saskatchewan. Interview and translation from Cree by Albert Angus.

41 Twenty-one days of Elders Focus Sessions were held between November 1997 and June 1999, to explore in greater detail some of the concepts and issues which Elders spoke about during nineteen days of Treaty Elders Forums co-hosted by the Federation of Saskatchewan Indian Nations and the Office of the Treaty Commissioner in the Fall of 1997.

42 Elder Peter Waskahat (Frog Lake First Nation, Treaty 6), November 15, 1997, FSIN Elders Focus Session, Saskatoon, Saskatchewan.

43 Elder Eli Adam (Fond du Lac Denesuline Nation, Treaty 8), November 5, 1997, Treaty Elders Forum, Fond du Lac, Saskatchewan.

44 Elder George Rider (Carry the Kettle First Nation, Treaty 4), September 15, 1997, Treaty Elders Forum, Wapii-Moostoosis Reserve, Lebret, Saskatchewan.

45 Elder Norman Sunchild (Thunderchild First Nation, Treaty 6), November 12, 1997, Treaty Elders Forum, Jackfish Lake Lodge, Cochin, Saskatchewan.

46 Elder Danny Musqua (Keeseekoose First Nation, Treaty 4), FSIN Elders Focus Session, Saskatoon, Saskatchewan.

47 Elder Dolly Neapetung (Yellow Quill First Nation, Treaty 4), September 15, 1997, Treaty Elders Forum, Wapii-Moostoosis Reserve, Lebret, Saskatchewan. Translated from Saulteaux.

48 Elder Jacob Bill (Pelican Lake First Nation, Treaty 6), November 14, 1997, Treaty Elders Forum, Jackfish Lake Lodge, Cochin, Saskatchewan.

49 Elder Danny Musqua (Keeseekoose First Nation, Treaty 4), September 4, 1997, Treaty Table Meeting 7, Office of the Treaty Commissioner, Saskatoon, Saskatchewan.

50 Elder Jimmy Myo (Moosomin First Nation, Treaty 6), April 30, 1997, FSIN Senate Meeting, Jackfish Lake Lodge, Cochin, Saskatchewan.

51 Elder Kay Thompson (Carry the Kettle First Nation, Treaty 4), May 14, 1997, FSIN Indian Child and Family Services interview.

52 Victor Echodh (Acting Chief, Black Lake Denesuline Nation, Treaty 8), November 4, 1997, Treaty Elders Forum, Black Lake, Saskatchewan.

53 Elder Peter Waskahat (Frog Lake First Nation, Treaty 6), November 12-14, 1997, Treaty Elders Forum, Jackfish Lake Lodge, Cochin, Saskatchewan.

54 Elder Jimmy Myo (Moosomin First Nation, Treaty 6), FSIN Elders Focus Session, Saskatoon, Saskatchewan.

55 Elder Danny Musqua (Keeseekoose First Nation, Treaty 4), September 3, 1997, Treaty Table Meeting 7, Office of the Treaty Commissioner, Saskatoon, Saskatchewan.

56 Elder Peter Waskahat (Frog Lake First Nation, Treaty 6), November 16, 1997, Treaty Elders Forum, Jackfish Lake Lodge, Cochin, Saskatchewan. Translated from Cree.

57 Elder Simon Kytwayhat (Makwa Sahgaiehcan First Nation, Treaty 6), December 21, 1997, FSIN interview, Saskatoon, Saskatchewan. Translated from Cree.

58 Elder Bart McDonald (Fond du Lac Denesuline Nation, Treaty 8), November 5, 1997, Treaty Elders Forum, Fond du Lac, Saskatchewan. Translated from Dene.

59 Elder Jacob Bill (Pelican Lake First Nation, Treaty 6), November 14, 1997, Treaty Elders Forum, Jackfish Lake Lodge, Cochin, Saskatchewan. Translated from Cree.

60 Elder Norman Sunchild (Thunderchild First Nation, Treaty 6), November 14, 1997, Treaty Elders Forum, Jackfish Lake Lodge, Cochin, Saskatchewan. Translated from Cree.

61 Elder Simon Kytwayhat (Makwa Sahgaiehcan First Nation, Treaty 6), December 21, 1997, FSIN interview, Saskatoon, Saskatchewan. Translated from Cree.

62 Elder Peter Waskahat (Frog Lake First Nation, Treaty 6), November 12, 1997, Treaty Elders Forum, Jackfish Lake Lodge, Cochin, Saskatchewan.

63 Elder Danny Musqua (Keeseekoose First Nation, Treaty 4), August 8, 1997, FSIN Elders Meeting, Wanuskewin Heritage Park, Saskatoon, Saskatchewan.

64 Elder Jimmy Myo (Moosomin First Nation, Treaty 6), August 8, 1997, FSIN Elders Meeting, Wanuskewin Heritage Park, Saskatoon, Saskatchewan.

65 Elder Alma Kytwayhat (Makwa Sahgaiehcan First Nation, Treaty 6), December 21, 1997, FSIN interview, Saskatoon, Saskatchewan. Translated from Cree.

66 Elder Jacob Bill (Pelican Lake First Nation, Treaty 6), November 16, 1997, FSIN Elders Focus Session, Saskatoon, Saskatchewan. Translated from Cree.

67 Elder Martin Josie (Hatchet Lake Denesuline Nation, Treaty 10), November 3, 1997, Treaty Elders Forum, Wollaston Lake, Saskatchewan. Translated from Dene.

68 Elder Norman Sunchild (Thunderchild First Nation, Treaty 6), November 14, 1997, Treaty Elders Forum, Jackfish Lake Lodge, Cochin, Saskatchewan.

69 Elder Peter Waskahat (Frog Lake First Nation, Treaty 6), November 12, 1997, Treaty Elders Forum, Jackfish Lake Lodge, Cochin, Saskatchewan.

70 Elder Gordon Oakes (Nekaneet First Nation, Treaty 4), November 27, 1997, Treaty Elders Forum, La Ronge, Saskatchewan.

71 Senator Allan Bird (Montreal Lake First Nation, Treaty 6), November 12, 1997, Treaty Elders Forum, Jackfish Lake Lodge, Cochin, Saskatchewan.

72 Elder Jimmy Myo (Moosomin First Nation, Treaty 6), March 23, 1999, FSIN Elders Focus Session, Saskatoon, Saskatchewan.

73 Elder Jacob Bill (Pelican Lake First Nation, Treaty 6), November 12, 1997, Treaty Elders Forum, Jackfish Lake Lodge, Cochin, Saskatchewan. Translated from Cree.

74 Elder Celeste Randhill (Fond du Lac Denesuline Nation, Treaty 8), May 22, 1997, Treaty Elders Forum, Nekaneet First Nation, Maple Creek, Saskatchewan.

75 Senator Allan Bird (Montreal Lake First Nation, Treaty 6), November 27, 1997, Treaty Elders Forum, La Ronge, Saskatchewan.

76 Senator Hilliard Ermine (Sturgeon Lake First Nation, Treaty 6), May 22, 1997, Treaty Elders Forum, Nekaneet First Nation, Maple Creek, Saskatchewan.

77 Elder Jacob Bill (Pelican Lake First Nation, Treaty 6), November 12, 1997, Treaty Elders Forum, Jackfish Lake Lodge, Cochin, Saskatchewan. Translated from Cree.

78 Elder Danny Musqua (Keeseekoose First Nation, Treaty 4), May 22, 1997, Treaty Elders Forum, Nekaneet First Nation, Maple Creek, Saskatchewan.

79 Elder Jacob Bill (Pelican Lake First Nation, Treaty 6), November 15, 1997, FSIN Elders Focus Session, Saskatoon, Saskatchewan.

80 Elder Peter Waskahat (Frog Lake First Nation, Treaty 6), November 15, 1997, FSIN Elders Focus Session, Saskatoon, Saskatchewan.

81 Elder Kay Thompson (Carry the Kettle First Nation, Treaty 4), January 15, 1998, FSIN Elders Focus Session, Saskatoon, Saskatchewan.

82 Elder John B. Bigeye (Black Lake Denesuline Nation, Treaty 8), January 15, 1998, FSIN Elders Focus Session, Saskatoon, Saskatchewan. Translated from Dene. Darryl McDonald, FSIN Treaty Governance Office, further explained that the term "Denesuline" refers to the "t" and "k" dialects which are spoken by different regions. The "people of the land" in the Athabasca region and Snowdrift, N.W.T. use the "k" dialect; some regions in northern Alberta and Manitoba speak the "t" dialect.

83 Elder Danny Musqua (Keeseekoose First Nation, Treaty 4), May 22, 1997.

84 Elders Jimmy Myo, Jacob Bill and Gordon Oakes, January 11, 1998, FSIN Elders Focus Session, Saskatoon, Saskatchewan

85 Elders Jimmy Myo, Jacob Bill and Gordon Oakes, January 11, 1998, FSIN Elders Focus Session, Saskatoon, Saskatchewan.

86 Elder Gordon Oakes (Nekaneet First Nation, Treaty 4), August 8, 1997, FSIN Elders Meeting, Wanuskewin Heritage Park, Saskatoon, Saskatchewan.

87 Senator Hilliard Ermine (Sturgeon Lake First Nation, Treaty 6), May 27, 1997, FSIN Elders Meeting, Wanuskewin Heritage Park, Saskatoon, Saskatchewan.

88 Elder Gordon Oakes (Nekaneet First Nation, Treaty 4), August 8, 1997, FSIN Elders Meeting, Wanuskewin Heritage Park, Saskatoon, Saskatchewan.

89 Elder Peter Waskahat (Frog Lake First Nation, Treaty 6), November 15, 1997, FSIN Elders Focus Session, Saskatoon, Saskatchewan.

90 Elder Celeste Randhill (Fond du Lac Denesuline Nation, Treaty 8), November 5, 1997, Treaty Elders Forum, Fond du Lac, Saskatchewan.

91 Elder George Cannepotato (Onion Lake First Nation, Treaty 6), November 12, 1997, Treaty Elders Forum, Jackfish Lake Lodge, Cochin, Saskatchewan.

92 Elder Gordon Oakes (Nekaneet First Nation, Treaty 4), April 29-May 1, 1997, FSIN Senate Meeting, Jackfish Lake Lodge, Cochin, Saskatchewan.

93 Elder Dolly Neapetung (Yellow Quill First Nation, Treaty 4), September 15, 1997, Treaty Elders Forum, Wapii-Moostoosis Reserve, Lebret, Saskatchewan.

94 Elder Danny Musqua (Keeseekoose First Nation, Treaty 4), May 22-23, 1997, Treaty Elders Forum, Nekaneet First Nation, Maple Creek, Saskatchewan.

95 Elder John James Mercredi (Fond du Lac Denesuline Nation, Treaty 8), November 5, 1997, Treaty Elders Forum, Fond du Lac, Saskatchewan.

96 Elder Bart McDonald (Fond du Lac Denesuline Nation, Treaty 8), November 5, 1997, Treaty Elders Forum, Fond du Lac, Saskatchewan.

97 Elder Bart Dzeylion (Hatchet Lake Denesuline Nation, Treaty 10), November 3, 1997, Treaty Elders Forum, Wollaston Lake, Saskatchewan. Translated from Dene.

98 Elder Kay Thompson (Carry the Kettle First Nation, Treaty 4), May 14, 1997, FSIN Indian Child and Family Services interview.

99 Elder August Lidguerre (Fond du Lac Denesuline Nation, Treaty 8), November 5, 1997, Treaty Elders Forum, Fond du Lac, Saskatchewan. Translated from Dene.

100 Elder Celeste Randhill (Fond du Lac Denesuline Nation, Treaty 8), November 5, 1997, Treaty Elders Forum, Fond du Lac, Saskatchewan. Translated from Dene.

101 Elder Louie Benoanie (Hatchet Lake Denesuline Nation, Treaty 10), November 3, 1997, Treaty Elders Forum, Wollaston Lake, Saskatchewan. Translated from Dene.

102 Elder Dolly Neapetung (Yellow Quill First Nation, Treaty 4), September 15, 1997, Treaty Elders Forum, Wapii-Moostoosis Reserve, Lebret, Saskatchewan. Translated from Saulteaux.

103 Elder Pat Robillard (Black Lake Denesuline Nation, Treaty 8), November 4, 1997, Treaty Elders Forum, Black Lake, Saskatchewan.

104 Elder Pauline Mercredi (Fond du Lac Denesuline Nation, Treaty 8), November 5, 1997, Treaty Elders Forum, Fond du Lac, Saskatchewan.

105 Elder Danny Musqua (Keeseekoose First Nation, Treaty 4), August 6-8, 1997, FSIN Elders Meeting, Wanuskewin Heritage Park, Saskatoon, Saskatchewan. Elder Musqua further explained that when he uses the word "heart" he means the "goodness and wealth" of the Crown.

106 The Canada Evidence Act. R.S.C., E-10, s. 20.

107 *R. v. Simon*, [1986] 1 C.N.L.R. 153, [1985] 2 S.C.R. 387, reversing [1982] 1 C.N.L.R. 118 (S.C.C.).

108 *R. v. Taylor and Williams*, [1981] 3 C.N.L.R. 114, 62 C.C.C. (2 d) 227 at para. 236.

109 *R. v. Taylor and Williams*, 62 C.C.C. (2d) 277 at para. 236.

110 *R. v. Badger*, [1996] 1 S.C.R. 771 at para. 52, [1996] 2 C.N.L.R. 77, (S.C.C), reversing in part [1993] 3 C.N.L.R. 143 (Alta C.A.).

111 *Delgamuukw* v. *British Columbia* [1997] 3. S.C.R. at para. 87.

112 *R. v. Marshall*, [1999] C.N.L.R. 161 (S.C.C.), rev'g [1997] 3 C.N.L.R. 209 (N.S.C.A).

113 *R. v. Badger*, [1996] 1 S.C.R. 771 at para. 41, [1996] 2 C.N.L.R. 77, (S.C.C), reversing in part [1993] 3 C.N.L.R. 143 (Alta C.A.).

114 *R. v. Badger* supra at para. 41.

115 *R. v. Sioui*, [1990] 3 C.N.L.R. 127, [1990] 1 S.C.R. 1025, 56 C.C.C. (3d) 225, 70 D.L.R. (4th) 427, 109 N.R. 22, 30 Q.A.C. 280 (S.C.C.).

116 Elder Jacob Bill (Pelican Lake First Nation, Treaty 6), June 24, 1999, FSIN Elders Focus Session, Saskatoon, Saskatchewan.

117 Elder Norman Sunchild (Thunderchild First Nation, Treaty 6), November 12, 1997, Treaty Elders Forum, Jackfish Lake Lodge, Cochin, Saskatchewan.

118 Elder Douglas Rabbitskin (Pelican Lake First Nation, Treaty 6), June 24, 1999, FSIN Elders Focus Session, Saskatoon, Saskatchewan.

119 In Cree vernacular, the term is also used to describe the time and place where the annual $5.00 treaty annuity is picked up.

120 Minutes of Proceedings of the Special Committee on Indian Self-Government, House of Commons, Canada, October 1983, at p. 12.

121 *Calder* v. *A.-G. of British Columbia*, 7 C.N.L.C. 91, [1973] S.C.R. 313, affirming 7 C.N.L.C. 43, (1970), 13 D.L.R. (3d) 64, 74 W.W.R. 481 (B.C.C.A).

122 Elder Alfred Billette (Buffalo River Denesuline Nation, Treaty 10), March 28, 2000, FSIN Elders Focus Session, Saskatoon, Saskatchewan.

123 "Report of Commissioner for Treaty No. 8," in *Treaty No. 8 made June 21, 1899 and Adhesions, Reports, etc.* (Ottawa: Queen's Printer, 1966).

124 Elder Danny Musqua (Keeseekoose First Nation, Treaty 4), August 8, 1997, FSIN Elders Meeting, Wanuskewin Heritage Park, Saskatoon, Saskatchewan.

125 Elder Kay Thompson (Carry the Kettle First Nation, Treaty 4), May 14, 1997, FSIN interview.

126 Elder Gordon Oakes (Nekaneet First Nation, Treaty 4), August 16, 1997, FSIN Elders Meeting, Saskatoon, Saskatchewan.

127 Elder Jimmy Myo (Moosomin First Nation, Treaty 6), August 6, 1997, FSIN Elders Meeting, Wanuskewin Heritage Park, Saskatoon, Saskatchewan.

128 Elder Kay Thompson (Carry the Kettle First Nation, Treaty 4), September 16, 1997, Treaty Elders Forum, Wapii-Moostoosis Reserve, Saskatchewan.

129 Elder Gordon Oakes (Nekaneet First Nation, Treaty 4), April 30, 1997, FSIN Senate Meeting, Jackfish Lake Lodge, Cochin, Saskatchewan.

130 Elder Gordon Oakes (Nekaneet First Nation, Treaty 4), April 30, 1997, FSIN Senate Meeting, Jackfish Lake Lodge, Cochin, Saskatchewan.

131 Senator Allan Bird (Montreal Lake First Nation, Treaty 6), November 28, 1997, Treaty Elders Forum, La Ronge, Saskatchewan.

132 Elder August Lidguerre (Fond du Lac Denesuline Nation, Treaty 8), November 5, 1997, Treaty Elders Forum, Fond du Lac, Saskatchewan. Translated from Dene.

133 Elder Norbert Fern (Fond du Lac Denesuline Nation, Treaty 8), November 5, 1997, Treaty Elders Forum, Fond du Lac, Saskatchewan. Translated from Dene.

134 Elder Joe Crowe (Kahkewistahaw First Nation, Treaty 4), April 30, 1997, FSIN Senate Meeting, Jackfish Lake Lodge, Cochin, Saskatchewan.

135 Elder John James Mercredi (Fond du Lac Denesuline Nation, Treaty 8), November 5, 1997, Treaty Elders Forum, Fond du Lac, Saskatchewan. Translated from Dene.

136 Elder Danny Musqua (Keeseekoose First Nation, Treaty 4), May 22, 1997, Treaty Elders Forum, Nekaneet First Nation, Maple Creek, Saskatchewan.

137 Elder Danny Musqua (Keeseekoose First Nation, Treaty 4), May 22, 1997, Treaty Elders Forum, Nekaneet First Nation, Maple Creek, Saskatchewan.

138 Elder Kay Thompson (Carry the Kettle First Nation, Treaty 4), September 14, 1997, Treaty Elders Forum, Fort Qu'Appelle, Saskatchewan.

139 See, for example, Arthur J. Ray, Sarah Carter, and Frank Tough.

140 Senator Allan Bird (Montreal Lake First Nation, Treaty 6), November 27, 1997, Lac la Ronge, Saskatchewan.

Glossary of Terms*

Ade Wakan Tunga
    An Assiniboine/Nakoda term meaning "sacred"

Anina Ombi
    An Assiniboine/Nakoda term describing themselves as "silent people"

Anishinabe
    A Saulteaux/Ojibway term describing themselves as the First People that came down from the Creator; coming down to be men/man

askiy
[us-SKEE]
    earth; land

askîwipimâcihowascikêwina
[us-SKEE-wi-PI-maa-TSI-hoe-WUS-tsi-KAY-wi-nuh]
    setting into place arrangements for livelihood

atoskêwimahcihowin
[uh-TO-skay-WI-muh-TIS-ho-win]
    an inner desire or need to work

atoskêwin
[uh-TO-skay-win]
    work; employment

Denesuline
    A Dene term describing themselves as "the people," or "the real people"

ê-miciminitômakahki
[AY-mi-TSI-min-NIT-toe-MUK-Kuhk-Ki]
    They are interconnected.

ê-wîtaskêmâcik
[AAY-wee-TUS-Kay-MAA-tsik]
    They live harmoniously and peacefully with them.

---

* For Cree words, pronunciations are given in square brackets.

itêyimikosiwiyêcikêwina
[i-TAY-yi-MI-KO-SO-wi-AY-tsi-KAY-wi-nah]
    arrangements ordained or inspired by our Father [Creator]

iyiniw miyikowisowina
[EE-yi-niw MEE-yik-KO-wis-SO-wi-nah]
    what has been given to the peoples

iyiniw sawêyihtâkosiwina
[EE-yi-niw SU-way-YIH-toa-KOS-si-wi-nah]
    the peoples' sacred gifts from the Creator

iyiniwak
[ee-YIN-ni-wuk]
    people made healthy by the land

iyiniwi-ministik
[EE-yi-NI-wi-MI-nis-stik]
    The Peoples' Island

iyinîsiwin
[EE-yi-NEES-so-win]
    ability to develop a keen mind

kakâyiwâtisiwin
[KU-Kaa-YI-waa-TIS-so-win]
    ability to develop an inner sense of industriousness or inner ability or desire to be hardworking

kakêskihkêmowina
[KUK-Kay-SKIH-Kay-MOE-wi-nah]
    teachings; counsel

kanâtisiwin
[KUN-naa-TIS-si-win]
    cleanliness

kiciwâminawak
[Ki-TSI-waa-MI-na-wak]
    Our cousins (yours and mine)

kihci-asotamâtowin
[Keeh-TSI-us-SOO-tu-MAA-toe-win]
 sacred promises to one another

kisêwâtisiwin
[Kis-SAY-waa-TIS-si-win]
 kindness; inner capacity to be kind

kwayaskâtisiwin
[Kwu-YUS-skaa-TIS-si-win]
 honesty and fairness

manâcihitowin
[MUN-naa-tsi-HIT-toe-win]
 act of treating each other with care and respect

manâtisiwin
[MUN-naa-TIS-so-win]
 inner capacity to respect; the act of being respectful

mâmitonêyihcikan
[MAA-mit-TOE-nay-YIH-chi-Kun]
 mind; intellect

Metah Koyabi
 An Assiniboine/Nakoda term meaning "all my relations"

miskâsowin
[mis-SKAA-soo-win]
 finding one's sense of origin and belonging; finding "one's self" or "one's centre"

miyo-wîcêhtowin
[mi-YOH-wee-TSAY-too-win]
 having or possessing good relations with one another individually or collectively

nahâsiwin
[nu-HAA-so-win]
 ability to develop alert and discerning faculties

Nakoda
 An Assiniboine/Nakoda term describing all the people

nahihtamowin
[NU-hee-TU-moe-win]
 ability to develop a keen sense of hearing

nêhiyawak
[nay-hi-yu-wuk]
 People of the Four Directions

niciwâm
[NI-tsi-waam]
 first cousin; son of maternal aunt or paternal uncle; parallel cousin

nisitohtamowin
[ni-SI-toe-TA-moe-win]
 ability to develop understanding

nistamêyimâkan
[nis-STU-may-YI-maa-Kun]
 first-born or the one who first received our ways

okimâw miyo-wîcihitowiyêcikêwin
[O-Ki-maaw MI-yo-WEE-tsi-HIT-toe-WE-yea-TSI-Kay-win]
 agreements or arrangements establishing and organizing good relations or relations of friendship between sovereigns

okimâw miyo-wîcihitowiyêcikêwin, wîtaskê-osihcikêwin
[O-Ki-maaw MI-yo-WEE-tsi-HIT-toe-WE-yea-TSI-Kay-win, wee-TUS-Kay-O-see-TSI-Kay-win]
 agreement between the sovereign leaders to establish good relations and to live together in peace

oskâpêwisak
[OS-Kaa-PAY-wis-suk]
 Elder's helpers

otawâsimisimâwak
[oo-TU-waa-SI-mis-SI-maa-wuk]
 children of the Creator

pâstâhowin
[paas-STAA-hoe-win]
 divine retribution with grave consequences for breaking vows

pimâcihisowin
[pi-MAA-tsi-HISS-so-win]
 making a living for oneself

pimâcihowin
[PI-maa-TSI-ho-win]
 making a living

pimâtisiwin
[PI-maa-TIS-si-win]
   life

sawêyihtâkosiwina
[su-WAY-yih-TAA-Kos-SI-wi-nah]
   Creator's blessings

tâpwêwin
[TA-pway-win]
   speaking the truth with precision and accuracy

tipahamâtowin
[ti-PU-hum-MAA-toe-win]
   treating each other commensurately

tipêyimisowin
[TIP-pay-MI-so-win]
   freedom; liberty

tipiyawâtisiwin
[TI-pi-YOW-waa-TI-so-win]
   independence

tipiyawêwisowin
[ti-piy-YU-way-WIS-so-win]
   ownership; self-worth; treasure

Wadopana
   An Assiniboine/Nakoda term describing themselves as
   "canoe people"

waskawîwin
[wus-KUH-wee-win]
   inner energy to move or developing a sense of personal
   initiative

wâhkôhtowin
[wah-KOHT-toe-win]
   good relationship (of the First Nations, with the Creator
   and with one another)

wiyôhtâwîmâw
[WE-yoh-TAA-wee-maaw]
   father/Creator

wîcihitowin
[WEE-tsi-HI-toe-win]
   The act of helping one another. Here, it refers to the
   mutual assistance and respect between land and people.

Wîsahkêcâhk
[wee-SUHK-Kay-tsaahk]
   Grandfather Spirit in the Creation story

wîtaskê-osihcikêwin
[wee-TUS-skay-O-se-TSI-Kay-win]
   agreement or arrangement to live together in peace and
   harmony

wîtaskêwin
[wee-TUS-Kay-win]
   living harmoniously and peacefully with one another

wîtisâníhitowin
[WEE-tis-SAA-ni-HIT-toe-win]
   familial relationships (kinship)

yôspâtisiwin
[YOU-spa-TIS-si-win]
   gentleness

Bibliography

Abel, Kerry M., and Jean Friesen, eds. *Aboriginal Resource Use in Canada: Historical and Legal Aspects*, Manitoba studies in native history; 6. Winnipeg: University of Manitoba Press, 1991.

Anemaat, Louise. "Documenting Secret/Sacred (Restricted) Aboriginal History." *Archives and Manuscripts* 17 (1989): 37-49.

Asch, Michael. *Home and Native Land: Aboriginal Rights and the Canadian Constitution*. Vancouver: UBC Press, 1993.

Asch, Michael. *Aboriginal and Treaty Rights in Canada: Essays on Law, Equity, and Respect for Difference*. Vancouver: UBC Press, 1997.

Barron, F. Laurie, and James B. Waldram, eds. *1885 and After: Native Society in Transition*. Regina: Canadian Plains Research Centre, 1986.

Brown, George, and Ron Maguire, eds. *Indian Treaties in Historical Perspective*. Ottawa: Dept. of Northern Affairs and National Resources, 1979.

Calf Robe, Ben, Adolf Hungry Wolf, and Beverly Hungry Wolf. *Siksiká: A Blackfoot Legacy*, *Good Medicine series*. Invermere, B.C.: Good Medicine Books, 1979.

Canada. Dept. of Indian Affairs and Northern Development, John Leslie, and Ron Maguire. *Historical Development of the Indian Act*. 2nd ed. Ottawa: Dept. of Indian Affairs and Northern Development Treaties and Historical Research, 1978.

Cardinal, Harold. *The Unjust Society: The Tragedy of Canada's Indians*. Edmonton: Hurtig, 1969.

Cardinal, Harold. *The Rebirth of Canada's Indians*. Edmonton: Hurtig, 1977.

Carter, Sarah. *Lost Harvests: Prairie Indian Reserve Farmers and Government Policy*, McGill-Queen's Series in Native and Northern Studies; 3. Montreal: McGill-Queen's University Press, 1990.

Carter, Sarah. *Aboriginal People and Colonizers of Western Canada to 1900*, Themes in Canadian Social History. Toronto: University of Toronto Press, 1999.

Clark, Bruce A. *Native Liberty, Crown Sovereignty: The Existing Aboriginal Right of Self-Government in Canada*, McGill-Queen's Series in Native and Northern Studies; 4. Montreal: McGill-Queen's University Press, 1990.

Coates, Kenneth. *Aboriginal Land Claims in Canada: A Regional Perspective*. Toronto: Copp Clark Pitman, 1992.

Cruikshank, Julie. "Oral Tradition and Oral History: Reviewing Some Issues." *Canadian Historical Review* 75, no. 3 (1994): 403-418.

Daugherty, William. *Maritime Indian Treaties in Perspective*. Ottawa: Indian and Northern Affairs Canada, 1983.

Dickason, Olive Patricia. *Canada's First Nations: A History of Founding Peoples from Earliest Times*. 2nd ed. Toronto: Oxford University Press, 1997.

Dyck, Noel. *What is the Indian 'Problem': Tutelage and Resistance in Canadian Indian Administration*, Social and Economic Studies; no. 46. St. John's, Nfld.: Memorial University of Newfoundland. Institute of Social and Economic Research, 1991.

Erasmus, Peter, and Henry Thompson. *Buffalo Days and Nights, Western Canadian Classics*. Calgary: Fifth House, 1999.

Freisen, Jean. "Magnificent Gifts: The Treaties of Canada with the Indians of the Northwest 1869-70." *Transactions of the Royal Society of Canada, Series 5;* 1 (1986): 41-51.

Frideres, James S. *Aboriginal Peoples in Canada: Contemporary Conflicts*. 5th ed. Scarborough, Ont.: Prentice-Hall Canada, 1998.

Friesen, Jean. "Grant Me Wherewith to Make My Living." In *Aboriginal Resource Use in Canada: Historical and Legal Aspects*, edited by Kerry Abel and Jean Friesen. Winnipeg: University of Manitoba Press, 1991.

Fumoleau, René. *As Long as This Land Shall Last: A History of Treaty 8 and Treaty 11*. Rev. ed. Toronto: McClelland and Stewart, 1996.

Getty, Ian A. L., and Donald B. Smith. *One Century Later: Western Canadian Reserve Indians Since Treaty 7*. Vancouver: University of British Columbia Press, 1978.

Getty, Ian A. L., and Antoine S. Lussier, eds. *As Long as the Sun Shines and Water Flows: A Reader in Canadian Native Studies*, Nakoda Institute Occasional Paper; no. 1. Vancouver: University of British Columbia Press, 1983.

Gibbons, Roger, and J. Rick Ponting. "Historical Overview and Background." In *Arduous Journey: Canadian Indians and Decolonization*, edited by J. Rick Ponting. Don Mills, Ont.: Oxford University Press Canada, 2000.

Goehring, Brian. *Indigenous People of the World*. Saskatoon: Purich, 1993.

Hall, David J. "'A Serene Atmosphere'? Treaty 1 Revisited." *Canadian Journal of Native Studies* 4, no. 2 (1984): 321-58.

Hansen, Lisa F. "Chiefs and Principle Men: A Question of Leadership in Treaty Negotiations." In *The First Ones: Readings in Indian-Native Studies*, edited by David Reed Miller and Saskatchewan Indian Federated College. Saskatoon, Sask.: Saskatchewan Indian Federated College Press, 1992.

Hildebrandt, Walter, Dorothy First Rider, and Sarah Carter. *The True Spirit and Original Intent of Treaty 7*, McGill-Queen's Native and Northern Series; 14. Montreal: McGill-Queen's University Press, 1996.

Jarvis-Tonus, Jill. "Legal Issues Regarding Oral Histories." *Canadian Oral History Association Journal* 12 (1992): 18-21.

Jones, Dorothy V. "British Colonial Indian Treaties." In *The History of Indian-White Relations: Handbook of North American Indians*, edited by Wilcomb B. Washburn. Washington, D.C.: Smithsonian Institution, 1988.

Kelly, Gary. "Class, Race, and Cultural Revolution: Treaties and the Making of Western Canada." *Alberta* 1, no. 2 (1993): 19.

Leslie, John F., and Ron Maguire. *The Historical Development of the Indian Act*. 2nd ed. [Ottawa]: Treaties and Historical Research Centre, P.R.E. Group, Indian and Northern Affairs, 1978.

Lightning, Walter C. "Compassionate Mide: Implications of a Text Written by Elder Louis Sunchild." *Canadian Journal of Native Education* 19, no. 2 (1992): 215-253.

Lister, Rota. "The Importance of Native Oratory." In *The First Ones: Readings in Indian-Native Studies*, edited by David Reed Miller and Saskatchewan Indian Federated College. Saskatoon, Sask.: Saskatchewan Indian Federated College Press, 1992.

Little Bear, Leroy, Menno Boldt, and J. Anthony Long, eds. *Pathways to Self-Determination: Canadian Indians and the Canadian State*. Toronto: University of Toronto Press, 1984.

Mair, Charles, and Historical Society of Alberta. Edmonton and District Historical Society. *Through the Mackenzie Basin: An Account of the Signing of Treaty No. 8 and the Scrip Commission, 1899*, Western Canada Reprint Series; 6. Edmonton: University of Alberta Press, 1999.

Martin, Calvin, ed. *The American Indian and the Problem of History*. New York: Oxford University Press, 1987.

Miller, J. R. "Owen Glendower, Hotspur, and Canadian Indian Policy." *Ethnohistory* 37 (1990): 386-415.

Miller, J. R. *Sweet Promises: A Reader on Indian-White Relations in Canada*. Toronto: University of Toronto Press, 1991.

Miller, David Reed, and Saskatchewan Indian Federated College. *The First Ones: Readings in Indian-Native Studies*. Saskatoon, Sask.: Saskatchewan Indian Federated College Press, 1992.

Milloy, John S. *The Plains Cree: Trade, Diplomacy, and War, 1790-1870*. Winnipeg: University of Manitoba Press, 1988.

Milloy, John S. "The Early Indian Acts: Developmental Strategy and Constitutional Change." In *Sweet Promises: A Reader on Indian-White Relations in Canada*, edited by J. R. Miller, 145-154. Toronto: University of Toronto Press, 1991.

Momaday, N. Scott. "Personal Reflections." In *The American Indian and the Problem of History*, edited by Calvin Martin, 156-161. New York: Oxford University Press, 1987.

Morris, Alexander. *The Treaties of Canada with the Indians of Manitoba and the North-West Territories. 1880*. Reprint. Saskatoon: Fifth House, 1991.

Ortiz, Alfonso. "Some Concerns Central to the Writing of 'Indian History'." *The Indian Historian* (Winter 1977): 17-22.

Paper, Jordan. "Cosmological Implications of the Sacred Pipe Ceremony." In *The First Ones: Readings in Indian-Native Studies*, edited by David Reed Miller and Saskatchewan Indian Federated College. Saskatoon, Sask.: Saskatchewan Indian Federated College Press, 1992.

Ponting, J. Rick, ed. *Arduous Journey: Canadian Indians and Decolonization*. Don Mills, Ont.: Oxford University Press Canada, 2000.

Price, Richard. *Legacy: Indian Treaty Relationships*. Edmonton: Plains Pub., 1991.

Price, Richard, and Cynthia Dunnigan. *Toward an Understanding of Aboriginal Peacemaking*. Victoria, B.C.: University of Victoria Institute for Dispute Resolution, 1995.

Price, Richard, ed. *The Spirit of the Alberta Indian Treaties*. 3rd ed. Edmonton: University of Alberta Press, 1999.

Purich, Donald J. *Our Land: Native Rights in Canada*, Canadian Issues Series. Toronto: Lorimer, 1986.

Pylypchuk, Mary Ann. "The Value of Aboriginal Records as Legal Evidence in Canada: An Examination of Sources." *Archivaria* 32 (1991): 51-77.

Ray, Arthur J. *Indians in the Fur Trade: Their Role as Trappers, Hunters, and Middlemen in the Lands Southwest of Hudson Bay, 1660-1870.* 2nd ed. Toronto: University of Toronto Press, 1998.

Saddle Lake Indian Reserve. *O-Sak-Do: Treaty No. 6 Centennial Commemorative Tabloid, Saddle Lake Indian Reserve, Alberta, Canada – July 1976,* 1976.

Surtees, Robert J. "The Development of an Indian Reserve Policy in Canada." *Ontario History* 61: 87-98.

Surtees, Robert J. "Canadian Indian Policies." In *Handbook of North American Indians – History of Indian-White Relations,* edited by Wilcomb B. Washburn, 81-88. Washington, D.C.: Smithsonian Institution, 1988.

Taylor, John Leonard. "Canada's North-West Indian Policy in the 1870s: Traditional Premises and Necessary Innovations." In *Sweet Promises: A Reader on Indian-White Relations in Canada,* edited by J. R. Miller. Toronto: University of Toronto Press, 1991.

Titley, E. Brian. *A Narrow Vision: Duncan Campbell Scott and the Administration of Indian Affairs in Canada.* Vancouver, B.C.: UBC Press, 1986.

Tobias, John L. "Indian Reserves in Western Canada: Indian Homesteads or Devices for Assimilation." In *Approaches to Native History in Canada: Papers of a Conference Held at the National Museum of Man, October, 1975,* edited by D. A. Muise. Ottawa: National Museum of Man, 1977.

Tobias, John L. "The Origins of the Treaty Rights Movement in Saskatchewan." In *1885 and After: Native Society in Transition,* edited by F. L. Barron and James B. Waldram, 241-52. Regina: University of Regina. Canadian Plains Research Centre, 1986.

Tobias, John L. "Protection, Civilization, and Assimilation: An Outline History of Canada's Indian Policy." In *Sweet Promises: A Reader on Indian-White Relations in Canada,* edited by J. R. Miller, 127-144. Toronto: University of Toronto Press, 1991.

Tobias, John L. "Canada's Subjucation of the Plains Cree, 1879-1885." In *Sweet Promises: A Reader on Indian-White Relations in Canada,* 212-240. Toronto: University of Toronto Press, 1991.

Tobias, John L. "Canada's Subjugation of the Plains Cree, 1879-1885." In *Sweet Promises: A Reader on Indian-White Relations in Canada,* edited by J. R. Miller, 212-240. Toronto: University of Toronto Press, 1991.

Tough, Frank, J. R. Miller, and Arthur J. Ray. *Bounty and Benevolence: A Documentary History of Saskatchewan Treaties.* Montreal: McGill-Queen's University Press, 2000.

Tough, Frank. *'As Their Natural Resources Fail': Native Peoples and the Economic History of Northern Manitoba, 1870-1930.* Vancouver: UBC Press, 1996.

Treaty Seven Elders and Tribal Council, et al. *The True Spirit and Original Intent of Treaty 7.* Montreal: McGill-Queen's University Press, 1996.

Upton, L.F.S. "The Origins of Canadian Indian Policy." *Journal of Canadian Studies* 10, no. 4 (1973): 51-61.

Weaver, Sally M. *Making Canadian Indian Policy: The Hidden Agenda, 1968-70.* Toronto: University of Toronto Press, 1981.